Doggin' Cleveland

The 50 Best Places To Hike With Your Dog In Northeast Ohio

DOUG GELBERT

illustrations by

ANDREW CHESWORTH

Cruden Bay Books

There is always a new trail to look forward to...

DOGGIN' CLEVELAND: THE 50 BEST PLACES TO HIKE WITH YOUR DOG IN NORTHEAST OHIO

Copyright 2008 by Cruden Bay Books

Cruden Bay Books
PO Box 467
Montchanin, DE 19710
www.hikewithyourdog.com

International Standard Book Number 978-0-9815346-7-1

*"Dogs are our link to paradise...to sit with a dog on a hillside
on a glorious afternoon is to be back in Eden,
where doing nothing was not boring - it was peace."*
- Milan Kundera

Ahead On The Trail

Introduction

Cleveland can be a great place to hike with your dog. Within a short drive your canine adventurer can be climbing hills that leave him panting, trotting through impossibly green ravines, exploring the estates of America's wealthiest families or circling lakes for miles and never lose sight of the water.

I have selected what I consider to be the 50 best places to take your dog for an outing around Cleveland and ranked them according to subjective criteria including the variety of hikes available, opportunities for canine swimming and pleasure of the walks. The rankings include a mix of parks that feature long walks and parks that contain short walks. Did I miss your favorite? Let us know at *www.hikewithyourdog. com*.

For dog owners it is important to realize that not all parks are open to our best trail companions (see page 14 for a list of parks that do not allow dogs). It is sometimes hard to believe but not everyone loves dogs. We are, in fact, in the minority when compared with our non-dog owning neighbors.

So when visiting a park always keep your dog under control and clean up any messes and we can all expect our great parks to remain open to our dogs. And maybe some others will see the light as well. *Remember, every time you go out with your dog you are an ambassador for all dog owners.*

Grab that leash and hit the trail!
DBG

Hiking With Your Dog

So you want to start hiking with your dog. Hiking with your dog can be a fascinating way to explore the Cleveland region from a canine perspective. Some things to consider:

🐾 Dog's Health

Hiking can be a wonderful preventative for any number of physical and behavioral disorders. One in every three dogs is overweight and running up trails and leaping through streams is great exercise to help keep pounds off. Hiking can also relieve boredom in a dog's routine and calm dogs prone to destructive habits. And hiking with your dog strengthens the overall owner/dog bond.

🐾 Breed of Dog

All dogs enjoy the new scents and sights of a trail. But some dogs are better suited to hiking than others. If you don't as yet have a hiking companion, select a breed that matches your interests. Do you look forward to an entire afternoon's hiking? You'll need a dog bred to keep up with such a pace, such as a retriever or a spaniel. Is a half-hour enough walking for you? It may not be for an energetic dog like a border collie. If you already have a hiking friend, tailor your plans to his abilities.

🐾 Conditioning

Just like humans, dogs need to be acclimated to the task at hand. An inactive dog cannot be expected to bounce from the easy chair in the den to complete a 3-hour hike. You must also be physically able to restrain your dog if confronted with distractions on the trail (like a scampering squirrel or a pack of joggers). Have your dog checked by a veterinarian before significantly increasing his activity level.

🐾 Weather

Hot humid summers do not do dogs any favors. With no sweat glands and only panting available to disperse body heat, dogs are much more susceptible to heat stroke than we are. Unusually rapid panting and/or a bright red tongue are signs of heat exhaustion in your pet.

Always carry enough water for your hike. Even the prime hiking days of late fall through early spring that don't seem too warm can cause discomfort in dark-coated dogs if the sun is shining brightly. During cold snaps, short-coated breeds may require additional attention.

🐾 Trail Hazards

Dogs won't get poison ivy but they can transfer it to you. Some trails are littered with small pieces of broken glass that can slice a dog's paws. Nasty thorns can also blanket trails that we in shoes may never notice.

🐾 Ticks

You won't be able to spend much time in Clevland woods without encountering ticks. All are nasty but the deer tick - no bigger than a pin head - carries with it the spectre of Lyme disease. Lyme disease attacks a dog's joints and makes walking painful. The tick needs to be embedded in the skin to transmit Lyme disease. It takes 4-6 hours for a tick to become embedded and another 24-48 hours to transmit Lyme disease bacteria.

When hiking, walk in the middle of trails away from tall grass and bushes. And when the summer sun fades away don't stop thinking about ticks - they remain active any time the temperature is above 30 degrees. By checking your dog - and yourself - thoroughly after each walk you can help avoid Lyme disease. Ticks tend to congregate on your dog's ears, between the toes and around the neck and head.

🐾 Water

Surface water, including fast-flowing streams, is likely to be infested with a microscopic protozoa called *Giardia*, waiting to wreak havoc on a dog's intestinal system. The most common symptom is crippling diarrhea. Algae, pollutants and contaminants can all be in streams, ponds and puddles. If possible, carry fresh water for your dog on the trail - your dog can even learn to drink happily from a squirt bottle.

At the beach, cool sea water will be tempting for your dog but try to limit any drinking as much as possible. Again, have plenty of fresh water available for your dog to drink instead.

❧ Rattlesnakes and Copperheads, etc.

Rattlesnakes and their close cousins, copperheads, are not particularly aggressive animals but you should treat any venomous snake with respect and keep your distance. A rattler's colors may vary but they are recognized by the namesake rattle on the tail and a diamond-shaped head. Unless cornered or teased by humans or dogs, a rattlesnake will crawl away and avoid striking. Avoid placing your hand in unexamined rocky areas and crevasses and try and keep your dog from doing so as well. Stick to the trail and out of high grass where you can't see well. If you hear a nearby rattle, stop immediately and hold your dog back. Identify where the snake is and slowly back away.

If you or your dog is bitten, do not panic but get to a hospital or veterinarian with as little physical movement as possible. Wrap between the bite and the heart. Rattlesnakes might give "dry bites" where no poison is injected, but you should always check with a doctor after a bite even if you feel fine.

❧ Porcupines

Porcupines are easy for a curious dog to catch and that makes them among the most dangerous animals you may meet because an embedded quill is not only painful but can cause infection if not properly removed.

Outfitting Your Dog For A Hike

These are the basics for taking your dog on a hike:

- ▶ **Collar.**
  A properly fitting collar should not be so loose as to come off but you should be able to slide your flat hand under the collar.

- ▶ **Identification Tags.**
  Get one with your veterinarian's phone number as well.

- ▶ **Bandanna.**
  Can help distinguish him from game in hunting season.

- ▶ **Leash.**
  Leather lasts forever but if there's water in your dog's future, consider quick-drying nylon.

- ▶ **Water.**
  Carry 8 ounces for every hour of hiking.

🐾 *I want my dog to help carry water, snacks and other supplies on the trail. Where do I start?*

To select an appropriate dog pack measure your dog's girth around the rib cage. A dog pack should fit securely without hindering the dog's ability to walk normally.

🐾 *Will my dog wear a pack?*

Wearing a dog pack is no more obtrusive than wearing a collar, although some dogs will take to a pack easier than others. Introduce the pack by draping a towel over your dog's back in the house and then having your dog wear an empty pack on short walks. Progressively add some crumpled newspaper and then bits of clothing. Fill the pack with treats and reward your dog from the stash. Soon your dog will associate the dog pack with an outdoor adventure and will eagerly look forward to wearing it.

How much weight can I put into a dog pack?

Many dog packs are sold by weight recommendations. A healthy, well-conditioned dog can comfortably carry 25% to 33% of its body weight. Breeds prone to back problems or hip dysplasia should not wear dog packs. Consult your veterinarian before stuffing the pouches with gear.

How does a dog wear a pack?

The pack, typically with cargo pouches on either side, should ride as close to the shoulders as possible without limiting movement. The straps that hold the dog pack in place should be situated where they will not cause chafing.

What are good things to put in a dog pack?

Low density items such as food and poop bags are good choices. Ice cold bottles of water can cool your dog down on hot days. Don't put anything in a dog pack that can break. Dogs will bang the pack on rocks and trees as they wiggle through tight spots in the trail. Dogs also like to lie down in creeks and other wet spots so seal items in plastic bags. A good use for dog packs when on day hikes around Northeast Ohio is trail maintenance - your dog can pack out trash left by inconsiderate visitors before you.

🐾 *Are dog booties a good idea?*

Although not typically necessary, dog booties can be an asset, especially for the occasional canine hiker whose paw pads have not become toughened. Trails can be rocky and in some places there may be broken glass or roots. Hiking boots for dogs are designed to prevent pads from cracking while trotting across rough surfaces.

🐾 *What should a doggie first aid kit include?*

Even when taking short hikes it is a good idea to have some basics available for emergencies:

▸ 4" square gauze pads
▸ cling type bandaging tapes
▸ topical wound disinfectant cream
▸ tweezers
▸ insect repellent - no reason to leave your dog unprotected against mosquitoes and biting flies
▸ veterinarian's phone number

The Other End Of The Leash

Leash laws are like speed limits - everyone seems to have a private interpretation of their validity. Some dog owners never go outside with an unleashed dog; others treat the laws as suggestions or disregard them completely. It is not the purpose of this book to tell dog owners where to go to evade the leash laws or reveal the parks where rangers will look the other way at an unleashed dog. Nor is it the business of this book to preach vigilant adherence to the leash laws. Nothing written in a book is going to change people's behavior with regard to leash laws. So this will be the last time leash laws are mentioned, save occasionally when we point out the parks where dogs are welcomed off leash.

Low Impact Hiking
With Your Dog

Every time you hike with your dog on the trail you are an ambassador for all dog owners. Some people you meet won't believe in your right to take a dog on the trail. Be friendly to all and make the best impression you can by practicing low impact hiking with your dog:

🐾 Pack out everything you pack in.

🐾 Do not leave dog scat on the trail; if you haven't brought plastic bags for poop removal bury it away from the trail and topical water sources.

🐾 Hike only where dogs are allowed.

🐾 Stay on the trail.

🐾 Do not allow your dog to chase wildlife.

🐾 Step off the trail and wait with your dog while horses and other hikers pass.

🐾 Do not allow your dog to bark - people are enjoying the trail for serenity.

🐾 *Have as much fun on your hike as your dog does.*

The Best of the Best

- **DOG-FRIENDLIEST PARK**
  Towner's Woods

- **BEST CANINE HIKE TO A VIEW**
  Fort Hill Trail - Rocky River Reservation

- **BEST HIKE TO MEET OTHER DOGS**
  Sand Run Metro Park

- **BEST 1-HOUR WORKOUT FOR YOUR DOG**
  Adam Run Trail - Hampton Hills Metro Park

- **BEST CANINE HIKE TO A WATERFALL**
  Cuyahoga Valley NP - Blue Hen Falls

- **BEST BEACH TO HIKE WITH YOUR DOG**
  Lakeshore Reservation

🐾 ***BEST HIKE TO CIRCLE A LAKE WITH YOUR DOG***
Hudson Springs Park

🐾 ***BEST DOGGIE SWIMMING HOLE***
Grand River/Paine Creek - Indian Point Park

🐾 ***BEST RAIL TRAIL FOR YOUR DOG***
Ohio & Erie Canal Towpath Trail

🐾 ***BEST PLACE TO HIKE ALL DAY WITH YOUR DOG***
Hinckley Reservation

🐾 ***BEST 5-MILE HIKE WITH YOUR DOG***
Hemlock Trail/Castle Valley Trail/Squire's
Lane Trail - North Chagrin Reservation

🐾 ***PRETTIEST HIKE WITH YOUR DOG***
Holden Arboretum

🐾 ***BEST HALF-HOUR HIKE WITH YOUR DOG***
Nelson-Kennedy Ledges State Park

🐾 ***MOST HISTORIC HIKE FOR YOUR DOG***
Squaw Rock Loop - South Chagrin
Reservation

🐾 ***BEST HIKE THROUGH MEADOWS***
Cuyahoga Valley NP - Virginia Kendall Unit

🐾 ***PARK YOU WOULD MOST WANT DOGS
ALLOWED WHERE THEY CURRENTLY CAN'T GO***
Seiberling Nature Realm

No Dogs

Before we get started on the best places to take your dog, let's get out of the way some of the parks that do not allow dogs at all:

Alderfer/Oenslager Wildlife Sanctuary - Medina
Farmpark - Kirtland
Forest Hill Park - Cleveland
Hach-Otis Woods - Willoughby Hills
Headlands Beach State Park - Mentor
(*dogs are allowed on the paved sidewalk but can't go on Ohio's largest Lake Erie swimming beach so what's the point*)
Herrick Fen Nature Preserve - Streetsboro
Kent Bog State Nature Preserve - Kent
Mentor Marsh State Nature Preserve - Mentor
Nature Center at Shaker Lakes - Shaker Heights
Sandy Ridge Reservation (trails only) - North Ridgeville
Seiberling Nature Realm - Akron
Tinkers Creek State Nature Preserve - Aurora

O.K. that wasn't too bad. Let's forget about these and move on to some of the great places where we CAN take our dogs on Cleveland area trails...

The 50 Best Places To Hike With Your Dog Around Cleveland...

1

Cuyahoga Valley National Park
– Happy Days

The Park

Cleveland coal baron and indus-trialist Hayward Kendall acquired this property in the early 1900s to use as a hunting retreat. Upon his death in 1927 the property transferred to his wife, Agnes, with the stipulation that it would eventually become a park named in honor of his mother, Virginia. Agnes Kendall was not interested in the property and turned it over to the State in 1929.

During the Depression of the 1930s the Civilian Conservation Corps was based in Virginia Kendall Park constructing trails and building the rustic Happy Days lodge for urban children. The buildings were designed to harmonize with the natural pat-terns of the land using locally quarried sandstone and wormy chestnut.

The Walks

The primary trail system runs south from the Visitor Center, high-lighted by a mile-long band of 30-foot sandstone ledges. The *Ledges Trail* circles the rock formations on a wide footpath that doesn't require the

Summit County	
Phone Number	- (216) 524-1497
Website	- www.nps.gov/cuva/
Admission Fee	- None
Park Hours	- Sunrise to 10:00 p.m.
Directions	- *Peninsula*; from I-80 take Exit 180 and go south on SR 8. Turn right on SR 303 West to the parking lot one mile on the right.

Your dog will look forward to a stop at Ice Box Cave on a hot day.

crazy passages emblematic of some of its area cousins, making this trail suit-able for any level of canine hiker. Spur trails climb to the nooks and crannies and the top of the ledges, often with stone steps to ease your dog's journey.

The grassy hills in Kendall Park are a special treat for fetching dogs.

Still there are drop-offs here so rein in a rambunctious dog. You can also tkae your dog around a trio of easy loops that dip into a verdant creek valley and tour fragrant pine woods.

The national park trails continue across Truxell Road to the *Salt Run* and *Lake* trails. The *Lake Trail* is a gentle trip around Kendall Lake on a wide, wooded path. Head towards the dam area for the easiest access for your dog to get a swim. Athletic dogs will welcome the chance to challenge the hills of the *Salt Run Trail*. Steps buried in the slope ease the ascents but this trot is sure to set your dog to panting. These pretty woods serve up long views with little understory from a paw-friendly dirt trail. A short cut-off slices the 3.2-mile loop in half but chances are your dog won't vote to take it.

If you park in the Virginia Kendall Unit your dog will reach these hikes on mown grass trails across enchanting hills. Your dog will love these hills as much as the sledders after a snowfall.

Trail Sense: Trail maps are available, complete with distances. Signposts can be counted on to deliver you to the right trail at intersections.

Dog Friendliness
Dogs are welcome on this diverse set of hikes.
Traffic
These trails are conveniently located and popular in every season.
Canine Swimming
Kendall Lake fills the bill nicely.
Trail Time
Many hours to a full day.

2
Hinckley Reservation

The Park

In divvying up the Western Reserve among the original land speculators who bought it from the State of Connecticut, this land fell Judge Samuel Hinckley, of Northampton, Massachusetts. Before dying in 1840 the judge became wealthy selling off his vast Ohio land holdings.

One of those buyers was Robert Whipp who came from England in 1824 to graze cattle. He became a butcher and eventually acquired more than 2000 acres here. He became so rich that his second wife, many decades his junior, enlisted the help of her brother and another man to murder old man Whipp. The burly Englishman fought off his attackers. When he died in 1890 - of natural causes - his land was sold to pay debts. Much of it has been reassembled for Hinckley Reservation that spans more than 2,600 acres.

Medina County
Phone Number - (216) 635-3200
Website - www.clemetparks.com/visit/index.asp?action=rdetails&reservations_id=1011
Admission Fee - None
Park Hours - 6:00 a.m. to 11:00 p.m.
Directions - *Hinckley*; from I-77 take Exit 145 and head south on Brecksville Road, SR 21. Go west on SR 303 and turn left on Slate Road. To reach the park office make the next right on Bellus Road.

The Walks

Just about anything your trail dog desires is on the menu at Hinckley Reservation. For an easy warm-up there is an hour trip around Hinckley Lake, either on the paved multi-purpose trail or, better yet, on the clay-based *Hinckley Lake Loop Trail*. The water is in view less than half the time, however, but your dog can slip into the lake for a swim on the east side and at the boathouse.

Two separate sets of ledges and cliffs are standout attractions in the park. A short climb to one of the highest points in Northeast Ohio will bring you to the base of Whipp's Ledges where your dog can easily scale the

50-foot high rock cliffs. Keep control of your dog as you cross the top of the ledges that feature sheer, unprotected unprotected drop-offs. In the southern end of the reservation your dog can wander the mossy Wordens Ledges with rock carvings of religious symbols.

Your dog will look forward to a day of exploring the ledges and rock formations in Hinckley Reservation.

Athletic dogs will want to sign on for the hill-and-ravine trails of Hinckley's western section. These wide, wooded trails are seldom exhausting and frequently enjoyable.

Trail Sense: A color trail map is available and you will need it since the park, especially in the western hills, could use a few more signposts. You will get confused more than lost as long as you have a map.

Dog Friendliness
Dogs are permitted on all 25+ miles of trails.
Traffic
Horses share most of the trails in the western hills, where the foot traffic thins out away from the lake.
Canine Swimming
The streams in the park are suitable only for splashing but Hinckley Lake can be accessed for dog paddling.
Trail Time
Many hours to a full day.

3
Holden Arboretum

The Park

Albert Fairchild Holden was born in 1866, the third of Delia Bulkley and Liberty Holden's nine children. His mother was instrumental in founding the Cleveland School of Art, which later became the Cleveland Institute of Art. His father made a fortune in the silver mines of Utah and was the owner of Cleveland's major newspaper, *The Plain Dealer*.

After graduating from Harvard with a degree in Mining Engineering in 1888, Holden joined his father in the silver fields of Utah. He later bought the family mines and organized the United States Mining Company to consolidate his expanding interests. Soon he was smelting more ore than anyone in the country and founded the Island Creek Coal Company in West Virginia to keep his furnaces stoked.

Albert Holden died of cancer in 1913. An avid botanist, he planned to endow the Arnold Arboretum at his alma mater as a memorial to his 12-year old daughter who passed five years earlier but his sister Roberta Holden Bole convinced him that Northeast Ohio deserved a first-class arboretum of its own. Thus was eventually born Holden Arboretum on 100 acres donated by Mrs. Bole in 1931. Today's "tree museum" has grown into one of the world's largest, with 6,000 varieties of plants and trees spread over 3,446 acres.

Lake County

Phone Number
- (440) 946-4400

Website
- www.holdenarb.org/

Admission Fee
- Free for members; per person fee for visitors

Park Hours
- 9:00 a.m. - 5:00 p.m.; closed Mondays November 1 to March 31

Directions
- *Kirtland*; take Exit 193 from I-90 and head south on SR 306. Turn left on SR 615 and right on Kirtland-Chardon Road. Cross Booth Road and turn left into the park on Sperry Road.

The Walks

Most formal arboreta do not welcome dogs so it is a rare treat to be able to bring your dog to these trails. There are more than a dozen here, ranging from garden strolls to meadow romps to mature woodland hikes.

The trails curve pleasingly among the plantings, often visiting the edges of ponds. Energetic dogs will want to push to the park's extremities on the sporty *Pierson Creek Loop* and *Bole Woods Trail* that explores a stunning beech-maple forest, designated a National Natural Landmark. In the southern region the Conifer collection is a spectacle of evergreen wonder any month of the year. You

Wood sprites and animals were carved into the base of this fallen 275-year old red oak.

may be distracted by the beauty of the place and not notice as you hike but your dog can get quite a workout in Holden Arboretum, with several hundred feet of elevation changes.

Trail Sense: A detailed color map comes with each admission. Did I say detailed? It even tells you how many steps there are on the trail staircases.

Dog Friendliness

The park brochure proclaims that "We Love Dogs" and indeed your trail dog is allowed across the arboretum, save in the Holden Wildflower Garden. Mutt mitts are provided.

Traffic

Foot traffic only and the crowds thin considerably the deeper you penetrate the collections.

Canine Swimming

This is not a place for swimming and fetching but no one will object if your dog slips into one of the 26 man-made ponds on the grounds to cool off on a hot day.

Trail Time

As little or much as your dog wants - it would take two days to fully explore Holden's collections.

4
North Chagrin Reservation

The Park

Feargus Bowden Squire came from England and went into the oil business by partnering with John Teagle to form Teagle & Squire in 1865. In 1876 the company was swallowed by John Rockefeller and Standard Oil. Squire became a vice-president and was one of America's richest men by the time he retired in 1909.

Squire became enchanted with the mature forests of Willoughby Hills and planned to build a grand estate. By the 1890s he had erected a magnificent turreted gatehouse in the style of an English country manor. But that was it. Nothing more was ever built.

After Squire's death the family sold his estate to become the keystone for North Chagrin Reservation. A number of smaller farm properties were appro-

Cuyahoga County

Phone Number
- (216) 635-3200

Website
- www.clemetparks.com/visit/
index.asp?action=
rdetails&reservations_id=1002

Admission Fee
- None

Park Hours
- 6:00 a.m to 11:00 p.m.

Directions
- *Willoughby Hills*; from I-90 exit onto SR 91, SOM Center Road. Parking lots are available on both sides of the road. To reach Squires Castle go east on SR 6, Chardon Road and south on SR 174, River Road East.

priated through eminent domain until the new park totaled nearly 1,200 acres, forming a rectangle roughly five miles in perimeter along the Chagrin River's western bank. Today the reservation encompasses over 2,100 acres.

The Walks

Ironically, the shell of Squire's Castle is the lasting legacy of F.B. Squire's life in most people's minds rather than his work in building Standard Oil into the world's largest business. The gatehouse never provided entry to a great estate but it does serve as the gateway to a great trail system.

Step out the backdoor with your dog and you are greeted by wide, compacted gravel paths that sweep into a ravine decorated by a climax beech-maple forest. The A.B. Williams Memorial Woods was lovingly tended by the park's first naturalist and is a National Natural Landmark. The *Castle Valley Trail* rambles across the hills to connect with the *Overlook Trail* that descends into the heart of the forest, terminating at a valley overlook. A detour leads to a virgin stand of white pines southwest of the castle.

Squire's Castle has been stripped bare inside and is just an impressive hollow shell today.

Loop variations are endless in North Chagrin with connector trails and the *Bridle Trail* that clocks in at over 10 miles. The *Hemlock Trail*, for instance, can serve as a stand-alone canine hike, a loop with the bridle trail or a circumnavigation of the park with the *Castle Valley Trail* and *Squire's Lane Trail*. It skirts unguarded clifftops but the ravines in the park are more rounded than instant-drop-to-your-dog's-death walls.

In the southwest corner of the park the *Buttermilk Falls Loop* is a quiet leg-stretcher for your dog through light, second-growth woods with a stop at a cascading falls.

Trail Sense: Detailed color trail maps are available.

Dog Friendliness
Dogs are welcome to use these trails.
Traffic
This is a busy park and the wide, clean trails and varied terrain are especially attractive to runners.
Canine Swimming
While not a swimming dog's idea of paradise there are many opportunites to find a splash and cool off.
Trail Time
Many hours available.

5
Bath Nature Preserve

The Park

Raymond Firestone was the last of Firestone Tire & Rubber Company founder Harvey Firestone's five sons to serve in active management of the family business. Firestone began in the company after graduation from Princeton in 1933 by pumping gas and became president from 1957 to 1964.

Although tires made the family fortune (and landed Ray Firestone on the cover of *Sports Illustrated* in 1961) his abiding passion remained the horses that automobiles displaced in American life. He built a 750-acre farm here for his family and stable of 20 or so retired racehorses that he rode and jumped regularly.

After his death in 1994, Bath Township purchased part of the estate after a bond issue and the Bath Nature Preserve was opened to the public in 2001.

Summit County

Phone Number
- None

Website
- www.bathtownship.org/Parks%20folder/BNP%20page%20parks.htm

Admission Fee
- None

Park Hours
- Sunrise to sunset

Directions
- *Bath*; from I-77 take I-71 west and exit immediately onto Brecksville Road going south. Make a right on Ira Road to the park entrance on the left at 4160.

The Walks

Bringing your dog to the former Firestone estate is her chance to be a farm dog for the day. After opening with a romp through wind-swept grassy hills you are enveloped by the trail system that covers more than five miles. From here your options are many but your best play is to chart a course around the perimeter of the 404-acre park. Along the way you will pass a stone-free field stream where your dog can scramble down the banks for a refreshing splash, a low-lying wet pasture known as the Garden Bowl, cool pine groves and climax forests. The trail surface varies from grass to farm road to asphalt.

Bogs are freshwater wetlands found in northern glaciated regions that receive more rainfall than they lose through evaporation. The substrate is largely composed of organic peat, usually rainwater fed and low in nutrients. The bog in Bath Nature Preserve is a tamarack bog, populated by deciduous conifers also known as larches that shed their needles each winter. There are very few tamarack bogs remaining in Ohio and this one too may soon disappear. A tree census in the early 2000s found only six surviving tamaracks and a preponderance of invasive red maples that signal the acceleration of the bog into a woodland.

Don't miss the *South Woods Trail* where the soft, mossy dirt is about as paw-friendly a path as your dog is ever likely to trot. The hills of the former horse and cattle farm are big enough for a good sled ride but there are also long, flat stretches.

Nothing beats finding a farm pond on a hot day.

Trail Sense: A detailed, reliable park map is available onsite and at the website. Junction signs and trailhead markers direct you on the trail.

Dog Friendliness
Dogs are welcome on these trails.

Traffic
The *North Fork Trail* that is the main conduit across the old farm is multi-use and half the trails are, appropriately, bridle trails. Slip away onto the designated hiker-only nature trails for an almost certain solitary ramble with your dog.

Canine Swimming
The park features five ponds but the centrally located Garden Pond is the only one that will host a doggie swim in the warm weather. Ringed with vegetation, access can be iffy.

Trail Time
More than one hour.

6

James H. Barrow Field Station

The Park

Hiram College was founded by Christian Church members in 1850 as Western Reserve Eclectic Institute. James A. Garfield, 20th U.S. president, was a student, English teacher, and, in 1857–60, principal of the institute. The school became Hiram College in 1867.

James H. Barrow, Chairman of the Biology Department and long-time gardening enthusiast, established the Field Station in 1967 to provide Hiram College students with the opportunity to supplement classroom activities with hands-on learning experiences.

The buildings, animals, and natural areas of the field station's 360 acres, including over 200 acres of beech-maple climax forest, are maintained entirely by students.

Portage County

Phone Number
- (724) 295-3570

Website
- admission.hiram.edu/learn/barrow.html

Admission Fee
- None

Park Hours
- Sunrise to sunset.

Directions
- *Hiram*; from the college at the intersection of SR 82 and SR 305, go east on SR 305, East Wakefield Road. After 1.5 miles turn right on Wheeler Road to the Field Station on the right.

The Walks

It won't take more than a few bounds down the county lane-like opening to these hikes for your dog to realize he is in for a special treat. Unlike the wide, groomed pathways that dominate most of the Cleveland-area reservations the Field Station loops travel on traditional, pick-your-way hiking trails. In the dense forest your dog will delight in the anticipation of what's up ahead around the next turn.

There are two stacked loop trails under the leafy canopy, the 3.7-mile *North Loop*, marked in yellow, and the 2.4-mile *South Loop*, marked in green. There are just enough bumps and rolls to keep things interesting for your dog

Bonus

Without question, the greatest tree in America prior to 1900 was the chestnut. Rot resistant with fine-grained wood, the chestnut tree supported both vibrant wildlife populations and entire rural economies. It was estimated that one in every four trees in the eastern forests was a chestnut tree - some as old as 600 years. But in 1904 an Asian fungus was discovered in the Bronx Zoo in New York and the blight soon decimated the chestnut population.
By 1950 millions of acres of woodlands were left with dead, standing trees. The chestnut blight remains 100% fatal - young chestnuts may reach 20 or 30 feet but are doomed to succumb to the disease.
A specimen of this original prince of the American forest can be seen along the *South Loop*.

as the routes eventually wind down to meandering streams deep enough for your dog to find a cool swimming hole.

Although the forest is dominated by maple trees (actively tapped for sugaring), a diverse woodland community is identified by wooden signs. A short *Flood Plain Trail* and *Old Field Loop* on mown grass paths impart further education here.

Trail Sense: A detailed mapboard will get you started at the trailhead and signposts and mile markers will keep you oriented on these canine hikes.

Your dog can get an arboreal education while touring the Barrow Field Station; this chestnut tree is doomed to die, however.

Dog Friendliness
Dogs are welcome to enjoy these lively trails.
Traffic
Unless you run into a class or field trip, expect a mostly solitary journey with your dog. Bikes, horses and motorized vehicles are forbidden.
Canine Swimming
The wide streams provide plenty of splashing and pool deep enough for dog paddling.
Trail Time
More than one hour.

7
Brecksville Reservation

The Park

When the last glaciers retreated from Ohio they left seven distinct ravines in this area that was one of the first open spaces acquired after the establishment of Cleveland Metroparks in 1917. By the time the Harriet Keeler Memorial Shelter House (Keeler was a long-time educator in the Cleveland public school system and nature enthusiast) opened in 1929 the park already sported a 5.5-mile bridle path, a one-mile nature trail, three baseball diamonds, two boys' summer camps, ten miles of foot trails, and two swimming pools. The federal Civilian Conservation Corps set up camp here in 1935 and worked on trail construction and the rustic Brecksville Nature Center. Today, Brecksville Reservation is the largest of the 17-park Cleveland Metropark system with over 3,400 acres.

Cuyahoga County

Phone Number
- (216) 635-3200

Website
- www.clemetparks.com/visit/index.asp?action=rdetails&reservations_id=1006

Admission Fee
- None

Park Hours
- 6:00 a.m to 11:00 p.m.

Directions
- *Brecksville*; on SR 82, east from I-77 and west from I-271.

The Walks

Hills and forests are the attraction for canine hikers at Brecksville and the best route to lap up plenty of both is on the four-mile *Deer Lick Cave Loop Trail*. This canine hike is conducted almost exclusively on wide, groomed carriage paths that roll up and down but seldom oppressively. The journey exceeds the destination here, although the sandstone overhang that forms the cave is not without interest. This stretch of the trail was the final leg completed in 1980 after more than twenty years building the *Buckeye Trail* that circles Ohio. The park features more than 16 miles of the *Buckeye Trail*.

Shorter loops are available to explore the ridges and streams that percolate the ravines. The *Hemlock Loop Trail* wanders under cool eastern hemlocks clinging to the Chippewa Creek Gorge and the paved *Prairie Loop Trail* introduces your dog to a tallgrass prairie.

Trail Sense: The trails are well-marked by signposts at junctions, a mapboard is available; color maps can be had in the Nature Center or printed from the website.

Small waterfalls like this one are a welcome find for your trail dog in the hills of Brecksville Reservation.

Dog Friendliness

Dogs are allowed on the trails across the park.

Traffic

Many of the footpaths are shared with horses but you can find long stretches of solitude at Brecksville.

Canine Swimming

Your dog will come across many streams and tiny waterfalls but probably won't find any deep enough for anything more than a refreshing splash.

Trail Time

Many hours available.

8
The
West Woods

The Park

These dark woods and sheltered rock outcroppings have long propagated rumors. Runaway slaves were hidden here on the Underground Railroad. Civil War soldiers sought refuge under the ledges. Bootleggers operated illegal stills in the hollows.

Homesteading in the late 1800s began to tame the wild lands and in 1933 W. H. Eisenman acquired 600 acres here as a retreat and place for maple sugaring. He eventually gave land here for his American Society for Materials headquarters.

The park began to take shape in the 1990s with donations and purchases by Geauga County. The 910 acres became The West Woods from an 1885 story by Albert Gallatin Riddle, a lawyer who took up writing in 1873 at the age of 57. Riddle's *The Young Sugar Makers of The West Woods* takes place in the area of this maple-beech forest.

Geauga County

Phone Number
- (440) 286-9516

Website
- www.geaugaparkdistrict.org/
parks/westwoods.shtml

Admission Fee
- None

Park Hours
- Sunrise to sunset

Directions
- *Russell Township*; on the south side of SR 87, 1.9 miles east of SR 306.

The Walks

The marquee canine hike among seven miles of trail in this Geauga County showcase park is *Ansel's Cave Trail,* named for Ansel Savage, an early 19th century settler from Massachusetts who may have squatted in the recesses of the sandstone ledges before obtaining land just to the west. This journey is conducted completely under tall straight hardwoods on wide, compacted stone paths. The trail moves easily up and across a ridge before dropping through a hemlock grove to the fanciful rock formations around Ansel's Cave. The full round trip covers 1.5 miles.

For more extended hiking with your dog the *Pioneer Bridle Trail* circles the wetlands and woodlands of Silver Creek for 2.7 miles. You can check out the horse trailer parking lot at the entrance on the way in to see if it is a busy horse day before setting out. Save some time for the short, paved interpretive trails around the Nature Center where your dog can cool down from the longer trails.

The Father of the Geodesic Dome, Buckminster Fuller, designed this one for the American Society of Materials.

Trail Sense: The trail junctions are marked by signposts and an excellent color map/brochure can be had on site.

Dog Friendliness

Dogs are allowed to enjoy these wooded trails and a pet hitching post is even provided if you want to visit the state-of-the art Nature Center.

Traffic

You won't see anything but foot traffic unless you venture onto the bridle trails.

Canine Swimming

The cold water Silver Creek is mostly deep enough only for trout.

Trail Time

More than one hour.

9
Nelson–Kennedy Ledges State Park

The Park

Retreating glaciers covered much of the prehistoric Ohio seabed with soil and rock but the formations at Nelson-Kennedy Ledges remained exposed. At the mercy of eroding winds and ice the sandstone cliffs have fissured and surrendered giant slump blocks of rock. In 1940 the State of Ohio began acquiring land in the area and in 1949 the park was created to protect the one-of-a-kind landscape.

The Walks

Your dog's hiking day here will be confined entirely to the Ledges that run north-south in a confined area that is bracketed by waterfalls at either end. Four color-coded trails fan out from the same trailhead opposite the south end of the parking lot. Following the prescribed routes can be difficult and it will take a few false turns before you get used to picking up the trail blazes. Or you can also disregard the trails altogether and let your dog investigate the rock formations and slot canyons as she will.

The *Yellow Trail* is the only one of the quartet that heads north, poking through slender passages at the base of the cliff wall on its way to Cascade Falls that plunge across a vertical rock face. Gold Hunter's Cave under the falls was the site of a brief and fruitless gold rush in the 1870s.

The southbound trails each offer a unique Ledge experience. The easy-going *White Trail* ascends to the top of the Ledges and morphs into a traditional woodland canine hike. It climaxes at two-tiered Minnehaha Falls where Sylvan Creek slides into a twisting canyon.

Portage County

Phone Number
- (440) 564-2279

Website
-www.dnr.state.oh.us/parks/tabid/775/Default.aspx

Admission Fee
- None

Park Hours
- One half hour before sunrise to one half hour after sunset

Directions
- *Garrettsville*; northeast of town on Nelson Ledge Road (SR 282), north of SR 305 and south of US 422.

The *Blue Trail* traverses the front of the Ledges and is the best route to view their striking natural beauty. Several species of ferns cling to the ledgess and the cool, moist rocks breed spectacular wildflowers such as the rare red trillium in spring.

Adventurous dogs will want to challenge the *Red Trail* that descends imaginatively into the heart of the Ledges. Don't be ashamed to

Going through Dwarf's Pass on all fours may be your best option.

turn back trying to follow your dog's wagging tail into seemingly impossible passages like Fat Man's Peril and the Squeeze. Eventually you pop out in the dark chill of the Devil's Icebox.

Trail Sense: Trail markings can be hard to decipher and brochures are unlikely to be stocked at the trailhead. If you can pre-print a map from the website, by all means do so.

Dog Friendliness

Dogs are allowed to test these rock passages.

Traffic

Foot traffic only.

Canine Swimming

Some splashing available in Sylvan Creek in the Devil's Icebox.

Trail Time

Allow more than one hour to fully explore the Ledges.

10
Cascade Valley Park

The Park

Akron was founded by Simon Perkins on the new Ohio & Erie Canal in 1825. In 1833, Dr. Eliakim Crosby, a one-time Connecticut schoolteacher and Army surgeon during the War of 1812, started a town just to north after building the Cascade Race, a waterway that powered mills and businesses along the canal. He called the town Cascade but the locals called it north Akron and it was absorbed into Akron three years later.

Next Crosby set his sights on the Cuyahoga River, buying up land to build a manufacturing center that he claimed would rival the most prosperous of New England. This new waterway, the Chuckery Race, filled in 1844 but financial reversals doomed the project. Dr. Crosby moved on to Wisconsin where he would die in 1854 at the age of 75. Traces of the historic Chuckery Race can still be seen in the park.

In the late 1970s, Metro Parks and the City of Akron developed a plan to transform 1,500 acres of land in the Cuyahoga River and Little Cuyahoga River valleys into a unique urban park called Cascade Valley with seven activity areas.

Summit County

Phone Number
- (330) 865-8060

Website
- www.summitmetroparksorg/ParksAndTrails/CascadeValleySouth.aspx

Admission Fee
- None

Park Hours
- 6:00 a.m. to 11:00 p.m.

Directions
- *Akron*; from SR 8 exit at Tallmadge Avenue. Go west for one mile to Cuyahoga Street. Turn right and the Chuckery entrance will be 3/4 mile on the right; the Oxbow area another 1/4 mile on the right and the Schumacher Valley Area further along on the left.

The Walks

Your dog can get a different hiking experience from each of the Cascade Valley activity areas. Oxbow and Chuckery brings the twisting Cuyahoga River into play from each side. Oxbow is primarily a recreational destination but serves up a wooded mile with a valley overlook thrown in. The sledding hill here makes this a popular spot in winter as well. Chuckery is more of a hiking spot for your dog with an hour ramble on a wide path that traces the Cuyahoga as it makes one of its sharper turns. If you want to make it an afternoon with your dog here, the *Chuckery Trail* links to the *Highbridge Trail* that leads to Gorge Metro Park 3.2 miles away. Steps in each area ease the harder climbs but there is nothing here that will wipe the wag off your dog's tail.

The Schumacher Valley Area, donated by descendants of German emigrant Ferdinand Schumacher, Akron's "Oatmeal King," is billed by the Park District as the "wildest terrain within the City of Akron." Indeed, these quiet woods harbor a quick descent into a steep-cut peninsula carved by tributaries of the Cuyahoga River. A slower, more gradual ascent closes the 1.2-mile loop that will sap the energy of the most energetic dog. As is the want in Cascade Valley Park, the *Schumacher Trail* can serve as a stand-alone canine hike or a warm-up for the 2.8-mile *Valley Link* that crosses the Cuyahoga River to the *Ohio & Erie Canal Towpath Trail* and even Sand Run Metro Park.

Trail Sense: Each area features only one trail, aside from links to other parks; maps posted at information kiosks and signposts at junctions should be sufficient to get you around but park map/brochures are also available onsite and online.

Dog Friendliness
Dogs are welcome to hike the trails but stay off the ballfields.
Traffic
The Schumacher Valley Area is the place to go to enjoy the woods alone with your dog although the trails get less play than the ballfields in the other areas. The *Chuckery Trail* can be used by cross-country skiers.
Canine Swimming
There is dog paddling afoot in the Cuyahoga River.
Trail Time
Up to an hour in any one Cascade Valley area or you can stay all day.

Cuyahoga Valley National Park – Hunt Farm

The Park

In 1974 Congress created the Cuyahoga Valley National Recreation Area as an urban park for the national park system, knitting together local parks and farmsteads that peppered the riverscape. Hunt Farm retains the feel of the small family farm with agricultural exhibits.

Hearby, two such farms have been donated in the park for public use, both owned and administered by Summit County MetroParks. O'Neil Woods was once the cattle farm of William O'Neil, founder of General Tire and Rubber Company. The 162 acres of woods and ravines in Hampton Hills served as farmland for a succession of families dating to the early 1800s.

Summit County
Phone Number - (216) 524-1497
Website - www.nps.gov/cuva/
Admission Fee - None
Park Hours - Sunrise to 10:00 p.m.
Directions - *Cuyahoga Falls*; on Bolanz Road about 3/10 of a mile west of Akron-Peninsula Road and 1/10 of a mile east of Riverview Road. O'Neil Woods is on the west side of the river on Martin Road, south of Ira Road. Hampton Hills is on the east side of the river east of Akron-Peninsula Road. Both are south of Hunt Farm.

The Walks

The *Deer Run Trail* through O'Neil Woods is two completely different hikes on one two-mile loop trail. The north side of West Beth Road (this hike requires two road crossings with your dog) tackles a steep hill, including a LONG staircase on the east side of the loop. Depending on your preference for stair-climbing take the loop counterclockwise to go up the stairs and down the natural slope or clockwise to take the wooden stairs going down. Across the road the trail flattens out and meanders beside the stream, crosses meadows and sweeps past an alder swamp.

The trail system at Hampton Hills is a stacked loop that climbs steadily up a ravine cut by Adam Run Stream and its tributaries. The full loop on the *Adam Run Trail* covers 3.2 miles or you can opt to take your dog on the 1.6-

mile *Spring Hollow Trail* sampler. The wide, dirt path makes a super hiking surface for your dog and the woodlands are fetching (look for a pine grove planted by the Girl Scouts when the park was opened in 1968) but Adams Run is not an attractive stream. The downed trees clogging the waterways won't concern your dog, however - he'll give this ramble high marks.

After climbing the hills of O'Neil Woods your dog deserves a break in the spa-like stream.

Trail Sense: Park maps are available and signposts reliably point the way. You won't need to follow your dog's nose here.

Dog Friendliness

Dogs are allowed on these trails; there is a grassy area for a game of fetch at the Hampton Hills parking lot.

Traffic

No bikes or horses allowed on these trails and there is enough climbing that casual walkers don't come here.

Canine Swimming

There is plenty of access to streams but more for cooling off than swimming.

Trail Time

Allow at least one hour in either O'Neil Woods or Hampton Hills.

12
South Chagrin Reservation

The Park

The Chagrin River that dominates the park was designated a State Scenic River in 1979. It is the only scenic river where the majority of its length is located within corporation limits. The river's name probably comes down from the local Erie Indian word for clear water - *shagarin*.

The first settler in this area was Serenus Burnet who brought his wife and little son to the west banks of the Chagrin in 1815. Not many others followed until the 1830s when James Griffith founded a village with a sawmill and quarry to extract Berea sandstone.

Griffithsburgh faded away but the quarry prospered. In 1877 the Chagrin Falls & Southern Railroad built a spur line to move even more rock. Finally in 1930 Cleveland Metroparks purchased this area and it has been quietly healing scars ever since.

Cuyahoga County
Phone Number - (216) 635-3200
Website - www.clemetparks.com/visit/index.asp?action= rdetails&reservations_id=1015
Admission Fee - None
Park Hours - 6:00 a.m to 11:00 p.m.
Directions - *Chagrin Falls*; from I-271 take Exit 26 East, Rockside Road, that becomes Cannon Road. After crossing US 422, turn left on Harper Road and right on Hawthorne Parkway into the park.

The Walks

South Chagrin serves up a panoply of short and mid-range hiking opportunites with your dog. The must-do routes here are down by the river where the *Squaw Rock Loop Trail* drops into the gorge, passes waterfalls run-ning over shale ledges and visits the rock carvings of Henry Church. Staircases take you in and out of the ravine but count on the footing for paws being wet and slippery.

Across the river, the *Squirrel Loop Trail* slips cautiously above the water under rock ledge sentinels. This route is for calm, well-behaved dogs only as steep drop-offs are unfenced. To close this loop you will need to take your dog along lightly traveled, but shoulderless Chagrin River Road.

The northern strip of park that hosts the polo fields is laced with flat, paw-friendly dirt trails. A real treat for your dog is a stroll on the *Sweetgum Loop Trail* through the park arboretum, one of the finest public tree museums of its ilk.

Trail Sense: A park map will need to be printed from the website before you arrive.

The carvings on Sqauw Rock are regarded as Henry Church's most famous work.

Dog Friendliness
Dogs are welcome to hike in South Chagrin Reservation.

Traffic
The hiking trails are likely to yield patches of solitude; runners favor the Polo Field trails.

Canine Swimming
There is access to the river in spots; Quarry Rock Picnic Area is a good one.

Trail Time
Any outing will last at least one hour with many possible.

13

Towner's Woods

The Park

From about 200 BC to AD 500, the Ohio River Valley was a focal point of the prehistoric Hopewell culture. These peoples were known for building impressive earthen mounds that were used for burials and ceremonies. Often times the tribal elders lived atop the mounds. Many mounds remain in Ohio, mostly in the southern part of the state but you can view one in Towner's Woods on the shore of Lake Pippen.

In 1932 an excavation of the mound took place and 11 skeletal remains were reported to have been uncovered, along with beads and other artifacts. One of the remains was rumored to be those of an Indian princess.

With European settlement came clearing of this land for pasturing and George B. Towner opened sand and gravel pits were here. In 1973 Portage County purchased land from the Towner and Bringham families to create its first park. Structures in the 175-acre park, including gazebos, benches and several picnic shelters, were constructed from recycled railroad materials.

Portage County
Phone Number - (330) 297-7728
Website - www.portageparkdistrict.org/
Admission Fee - None
Park Hours - Dawn to dusk
Directions - *Ravenna*; from SR 44 take SR 59 west in the center of town. Turn right on Brady Lake Road and follow to Ravenna Road on the right. Cross the railroad tracks and turn right into the park.

The Walks

Towner's Woods used to be a true paradise for dog owners where dogs could hike under voice control - a park for dogs, not a dogpark. That ended on February 23, 2006 when off-leash prohibitions were enacted in the park. Still, there is plenty for your dog to love in Towner's Woods.

There are many short trail options and rolling hills to keep your dog alert for things to check out. The understory is skimpy so your dog will get long views through the woods. Along the *Lakeside Trail* those views include

fingers of Lake Pippen. Your dog will be tempted to bound down the hillside into the water but Lake Pippen is Akron City property and off limits. A rusty wire fence will dissuade any canine thoughts to the contrary. In Towner's Woods your dog will be trotting happily down soft paths, wide enough to understand why thes trails are highly favored by Nordic skiers in the winter.

Towner's Woods is also a jumping on point for the *Portage Hike/Bike Trail* that will one day wind 32 miles throughout Portage County. For now, canine hikers can travel several miles between Ravenna and Kent on this flat, often shady clay-and-limestone path.

Trail Sense: A reliable trail map is posted on an information board and can be printed from the website.

Dog Friendliness
Dogs are welcome in Towner's Woods and a water bowl can usually be found at the base of the old railroad switch tower beside the parking lot.

Traffic
Expect to find plenty of other trail users - many with a dog or two at the heel - in Towner's Woods.

Canine Swimming
Nope, hiking only in the woods.

Trail Time
An hour or more.

14
Sand Run
Metro Park

The Park

The Portage Path that runs through Sand Run Metro park was the primary Indian trail between the Cuyahoga and Tuscarawas rivers for crossing from Lake Erie to the Ohio River. In 1785 the Fort McIntosh treaty set the western boundary of the new United States as the Cuyahoga River.

That boundary persisted through the six years of Indian wars, and in 1796 the Cuyahoga River and the Portage Path Western boundary was again accepted. It would not be until 1811 and the Battle of Tippecanoe that the lands in Ohio west of the Cuyahoga and Portage Path started to be absorbed by the United States.

Summit County

Phone Number
- (330) 865-8060

Website
- www.summitmetroparks.org/ParksAndTrails/SandRun.aspx

Admission Fee
- None

Park Hours
- 6:00 a.m. to 11:00 p.m.

Directions
- *Akron*; exit I-77 at Miller Road and head east. Follow Miller Road until it dead-ends into Sand Run parkway. Turn right and cross Revere Road into park.

Opened to the public in 1929, Sand Run Metro Park was the first public park in Summit County. The Civilian Conservation Corps built many of its shelters and other park structures during the 1930s.

The Walks

The flat *Parkway Jogging Trail* that snakes along Sand Run for six miles is the most popular trail in Summit County, averaging more than 1,000 users a day year-round. Although hard by the Sand Run Parkway, this shady, hard-packed path does hold some charm for canine hikers.

Athletic dogs will want to head straight for the middle of Sand Run West and tackle the 1.8-mile *Dogwood Trail* that ducks into the woods and plows straight up a hill to a high grassy ridge. General Elijah Wadsworth used this ridge as a lookout during the War of 1812 when he camped in the present-day Old Portage Area of the park. Your dog's purchase for his exertion is a descent through a spooky ravine where trees clinging tenuously to slopes appear ready to fall around you. This route probably doesn't receive 1,000 trail users in a month.

A happy medium for dog owners is the *Mingo Trail* that circles Sand Run Stream for 3.3 miles, staying under majestic hardwoods much of the time and delivering an hour of spirited canine hiking.

Trail Sense: A park map is available and posted on kiosk boards. Several trails share the same path at times so pay attention to the directional signposts.

Dog Friendliness
Dogs are allowed on the trails across the park.

Traffic
This is the most-visited park in Akron but steer to the *Mingo Trail* and *Dogwood Trail* for quiet time with your dog.

Canine Swimming
Depending on when you visit, Sand Run Stream can be a diverting little flow or a torrent battling against its stone banks.

Trail Time
Several hours available.

15
West Branch State Park

The Park

The abundance of salt in this area attracted a rich bounty of wildlife that was harvested by early Delaware Indians who called the river draining the region "mahonink," meaning "at the salt lick." European settlers rapidly built industry along the Mahoning River.

At the West Branch, one of the Mahoning's main tributaries, the Flood Control Act of 1958 authorized the construction of the Michael J. Kirwan Dam and Reservoir as one of 16 flood control projects in the Pittsburgh District. Since its completion in 1965, the 83-foot high earth-filled Kirwan Dam has prevented flood damages estimated to be in excess of $488 million. The park opened the following year in 1966. Today, all sizes and types of watercraft are found boating on the reservoir - from cruisers and runabouts of unlimited horsepower, many with skiers in tow, to small fishing boats and canoes plying the coves and inlets in search of fish.

Portage County

Phone Number
- (330) 296-3239

Website
- www.dnr.state.oh.us/tabid/795/default.aspx

Admission Fee
- None

Park Hours
- 6:00 a.m. to 11:00 p.m.

Directions
- *Ravenna*; east of town on Rock Spring Road, south of SR 5 from SR 59.

The Walks

As much fun as there is on the water, your trail dog can find just as much on land. A series of wooded hiking loops connect to the campground on the north shore. The best of the lot is the *Wild Black Cherry* trail that rolls in and out of ravines as it hugs the lakeshore where your dog can find a way in for a swim. A satisfying one-hour canine hike from the campground can be stitched together with the *Deer Run Trail* and *Club Moss Trail*, natural paths all in the park's "No Hunting Zone." Ambitious canine hikers will want to test the 8-mile loop of the *Buckeye Trail* that traverses the western end of the reservoir.

Dog owners can also take advantage of 12 miles of mountain bike trails on the south shore that were originally developed as snowmobile trails. Over the years they have morphed into dipping and dropping single track. Rocks play a bigger role on these trails than on the north side, glacial till mostly. The *Rock Gorge Trail* is a highlight here, descending into a gorge with a flowing creek below and several very rocky sections. Lake views abound.

The Army Corps of Engineers maintains a nature trail, *Little Jewel Run*, located in the vicinity of the dam's outflow. In addition, there are also snowmobile, cross-country skiing and bridle trails available in West Branch State Park.

Trail Sense: Trail maps are available and trails are marked with blazes and signs but watch closely for blowdowns, many of which seem to have taken out a tree with a painted blaze.

Dog Friendliness
Dogs are welcome to hike the trails and stay in the campground.
Traffic
This is one of the closest legal mountain bike systems to the City of Cleveland that is accessed by Cable Line Road on the south side of the lake. But trail users are few and far between.
Canine Swimming
Absolutely - more than 3,000 acres of water when the reservoir is full.
Trail Time
A few hours to a full day.

16
Bedford Reservation

The Park

Bedford Reservation harbors Tinkers Creek Gorge where the stream ends its 30-mile journey to the Cuyahoga River by plunging a dramatic 220 feet over a course of two miles. The energetic water has gouged a steep, walled gorge that was inaccessible to homesteading or logging, securing its preservation as a unique natural area. The United States Park Service recognized as such and declared Tinkers Creek Gorge a National Natural Landmark in 1968. The stream is named after Joseph Tinker, the principal boatman for General Moses Clevealand's survey crew, who died in a boating accident on a return trip to New England.

The Walks

The canine hiking in Bedford Reservation is among the most spectacular in the Emerald Necklace. To fully experience Tinkers Creek Gorge you will need to go many miles on the *Buckeye Trail* and the park *Bridle Trail* if you want to create a loop of several hours duration. Experienced trail dogs only need apply.

For less adventurous dogs there are options to the attractions of Tinkers Gorge. The paved *All-Purpose Trail* travels along the rim, mostly flat and mostly shaded and affords views into the wooded chasm. In the east end of the reservation the *Viaduct Park Loop Trail* tours a mid-1800s stone viaduct and the powerful Great Falls of Tinker's Creek spilling over cracked ledges.

Cuyahoga County

Phone Number
- (216) 635-3200

Website
- www.clemetparks.com/visit/index.asp?action=rdetails&reservations_id=1000

Admission Fee
- None

Park Hours
- 6:00 a.m. to 11:00 p.m.

Directions
- *Bedford*; the park is situated between I-77 to the west and I-480/271 to the east.
Exit I-77 onto Pleasant Valley Road east to Dunham Road and turn left to the park office past Tinkers Creek.
From I-480/271 exit onto SR 14 east and turn right on Alexander Road to Dunham Road. Turn right and same.

Travel to the west end of the gorge and the *Hemlock Loop Trail* is an easy romp for any dog. There aren't many hemlocks but the route does allow fun splashing in the creek.

For a likely solitary outing with your dog check out the woods along Sagamore Creek. The loop here is an easy 90-minutes circling and tagging the stream several times.

Trail Sense: A trail map may be hard to find onsite but can be printed from the website and will be mandatory to find your way around this large park of over 2,000 acres.

Dog Friendliness

Dogs are permitted to hike throughout Bedford Reservation.

Traffic

Most of these trails allow horses but are not crowded velow the gorge rim.

Canine Swimming

Tinker's Creek Is elther too lively or too shallow to make it a prime doggie swimming hole.

Trail Time

You can check off the short trails in the park in a little more than an hour but most outings will be more like a half-day.

47

17
Gorge Metro Park

The Park

Local hardware store owner L.W. Loomis was the first to realize the power of the Cuyahoga River to lure tourists. In 1877 he began construction of open-air dance pavilions, low-swinging suspension bridges, boardwalks, skating rinks and a soon-to-be famous roller coaster for his new High Bridge Glens Park. The amusement center opened in 1882 and soon 60 trainloads and trolley cars of tourists were arriving daily. The hiking trail at that time led into the gorge crossed the river and headed back out the other side. Hikers also had the option of returning on the water via a somewhat harrying ride on a raft attached to guidewires.

Summit County

Phone Number
- (330) 867-5511

Website
- www.summitmetroparks.org/ParksAndTrails/Gorge.aspx

Admission Fee
- None

Park Hours
- 6:00 a.m. to sunset

Directions
- *Cuyahoga Falls*; west of SR 8. Exit onto Howe Road and turn right on Front Street. Cross the river and park in the lot on the left.

The amusement park operated for more than 30 years until the Northern Ohio Traction & Light Company constructed a dam at the Cuyahoga Falls that flooded part of the grounds and desecrated the scenery. In 1930 the utility company donated 144 acres for today's park.

The Walks

The marquee trail in the park is the *Gorge Trail* that loops through the valley above the spillwater from the 57-foot high Ohio Edison dam. This is an easy 1.8-mile round trip conducted on two levels. The highlight of the upper segment comes when your dog picks her way through a maze of jumbled rock ledges. Trail signs label this stretch as "difficult" and a bypass is offered but there is nothing here your dog can't handle. In fact, stone steps have been cut into the most troublesome passages.

The lower path meanders along the top of the gorge, affording views of the lively Cuyahoga River below. The clifftops are unprotected, however, and a fall here will not be pretty. A wooden staircase leads back out of the gorge. This entire hike is leafy and shady for your dog.

Two other trails are available at Gorge Metro; across Front Street the *Glens Trail* hugs the widening Cuyahoga River for nearly two miles and on the south side of the waterway the *Highbridge Trail* connects to Cascade Valley Metro Park 3.2 miles away.

Trail Sense: A park map/brochure is available and wooden posts mark trailheads and junctions.

Mary Campbell stayed in this cave when she became the first white child to settle, albeit against her will, in the Western Reserve.

Dog Friendliness
Dogs are allowed on the trails; look for a little stone drinking bowl with faucet on the *Gorge Trail*.

Traffic
Foot traffic only and it can get busy, especially on the trail to the deck overlooking the dam.

Canine Swimming
Along the *Gorge Trail* your dog can slip into the Cuyahoga River above the dam but keep close to shore; the swimming is easier from the *Glens Trail*.

Trail Time
More than one hour.

18
Swine Creek Reservation

The Park

Swine Creek Reservation began life as a massive 1,200-acre hunting preserve owned by Windsor Ford of Mesopotamia. In 1977 he sold 268 acres to Geauga County which included a pond and a lodge. Thirty acres are set aside as an active sugarbush and on "Sap's-A-Risin!" Sundays throughout March, the history of maple sugaring is displayed and demonstrated.

The Walks

More than six miles of trails in Swine Creek Reservation explore yawning ravines in an airy mixed pine and hardwood forest. The best way to start rambling with your dog is on the

Geauga County

Phone Number
- (440) 286-9516

Website
- www.co.geauga.oh.us/
departments/park_district/
swine_creek.htm

Admission Fee
- None

Park Hours
- 6:00 a.m to 11:00 p.m.

Directions
- *Hayes Corners*; at 16004 Hayes Road, two miles south of SR 87, east of the intersection with SR 528.

the *Wagon Trail* from which many of the shortish trails link as it completes its .8-mile loop. This wide, compacted gravel path provides superior trotting for your dog.

Well-worn natural single track drops down slopes cut by branches of the Swine Creek flowing into the mother stream. The *Valley Trail* is one of the hilliest while the *Squaw Root Trail* skirts the top of the ravine from behind the park lodge while visiting an aromatic pine plantation. You'll experience firsthand the namesake brown rock of the *Siltstone Trail* as you rock-hop across streams. Your dog 's four-paw drive will have no trouble but two-legged crossers need to take care on these slippery stones in the water.

The *Gray Fox Trail* is the park's longest loop at 1.2 miles and penetrates the heart of the leafy understory in the beech-maple forest that supplies sap for the Sugarhouse. These woods are agreeable enough that you will want to spend the afternoon checking off all 11 short trails in Swine Creek Reservation.

Additional trail time can be had off Swine Creek Road on property abandoned by the Baltimore & Ohio Railroad. Here the _Razorback Trail_ brings Swine Creek into play for your dog and spends time in open meadows.

Trail Sense: A map/brocure is available but may not be available on-site. There are no mapboards so this will leave you completely without orientation. The many trails are well-marked with directions and distances on signposts so come with a mind to explore and you will have as much fun as your dog.

Dog Friendliness
Dogs are welcome to enjoy these trails.

Traffic
You may encounter a trail user or two who has wandered away from the picnic shelters but seldom enough to make it seem like this is not your own private woods. The _Wagon Trail_ is multi-use; the others hiker-only.

Canine Swimming
Two fishing ponds, one at each end of the Y-shaped main parking lot, will get your water-loving dog's ears to perk up.

Trail Time
Less than one hour to a half-day.

19
Allardale

The Park

Stanley and Esther Allard donated 125 acres of a three-generation family farm to Medina County in 1992 "so others can enjoy the open spaces, the blue sky, the trees, the flowers, the birds and the hills and valleys that we have loved so much."

In the 1930s Allardale was one of the first farms in Northeast Ohio to practice soil-saving techniques such as contour strip farming and the planting of pines and spruces along steep hillsides. In fact, Stan Allard estimated that he planted over 100,000 trees during his lifetime.

Plantings continue apace today and Allardale is considered one of the finest tree farms in Ohio.

Medina County

Phone Number
- (330) 722-9364

Website
- www.medinacountyparkscom/
Pages/Allardale.html

Admission Fee
- None

Park Hours
- 8:00 a.m to dark

Directions
- *Remson Corners*; take Exit 3 from I-271 and go south on Ridge Road, SR 94, to Remsen Road. Turn left and travel east to the park entrance on the left, past State Road.

The Walks

Taking your dog around Allardale is like touring your own private estate grounds. A paved half-mile loop is tucked inside a mile-long, mostly grass path that climbs across a meadow to the top of Medina County's hilliest park and drops through a hardy beech-maple forest to a floodplain finish that is a wonder to behold during spring wildflower season. More blooms can be seen on the *Wildflower Trail* that ducks into an airy woods and travels around a shallow stream on a gravel path. Heck, your dog won't howl in protest if you decide to go round a second time.

Trail Sense: Park maps are available but just jump on the trail at the parking lot and leisurely follow it around.

On a hot day your dog may be more interested in shade than the view at Dedication Overlook.

Dog Friendliness

Dogs are allowed to hike around Allardale and mutt mitts are provided.

Traffic

Expect to share the Allardale loops with other walkers, often with a dog in tow.

Canine Swimming

The stream gurgles lightly and is an ideal sittin' and coolin' off stream but not deep enough for canine aquatics.

Trail Time

About one hour.

20
Chapin Forest Reservation

The Park

When this land of glacier-formed ledges and towering forests was threatened with logging after World War II, Frederic H. Chapin purchased 390 acres and turned it over to the the State of Ohio.

The park is especially popular during the winter when nordic skiers gather at the Pine Lodge Ski Center to take advantage of the groomed trails, fireplace and amenities. Storms blowing across Lake Erie clip the elevated ledges here and begin dropping the snow for which this part of Northeast Ohio is famous.

The Walks

Chapin Forest serves up more than five miles of trails to hike with your dog, mostly on the blue blazes of the *Buckeye Trail* that follows a serpentine route across the park. The most dramatic scenery under the majestic climax forest are among the ledges and rock outcroppings of Sharon conglomerate but these paths are restricted and open only to guided walks, which are scheduled regularly throughout the year.

First time visitors to Chapin Forest will want to take dogs on the 1.5-mile *Lucky Stone Loop*. Like most of the trails that wind through the mature woods, this wide path is formed from compacted stone and fine gravel and mostly paw-friendly. After a moderate, tongue-wagging climb to the top of the ledges the *Lucky Stone* rolls merrily along. The highlight comes at a break in the trees where the view on a clear day reaches all the way to Lake Erie and the

Lake County

Phone Number
- (440) 256-3810

Website
- www.lakemetroparks.com/select-park/chapin.shtml

Admission Fee
- None

Park Hours
- Sunrise to 1/2 hour after sunset

Directions
- *Kirtland*; take Exit 193 from I-90 and head south on SR 306, Chillicothe Road. The main park entrance is on the right at 10090 after crossing Eagle Road. An alternate entrance can be reached by continuing to Chardon Road, making a right and another right on Hobart Road.

Cleveland skyline about 18 miles away. There is no finer overlook in Northeast Ohio.

There are other half-hour canine hiking loops at either end of the park. You can also take your dog on any combination of small loops off the *Buckeye Trail* that acts as a spine to the mostly linear trail system. However you craft your dog's hiking day in Chapin Forest Reservation, you will be in no hurry to leave.

Trail Sense: Park maps are posted on information boards and can be printed from the website. Signposts point the way at trailheads and junctions and also indicate the level of difficulty of each trail.

Dog Friendliness

Dogs are welcome throughout Chapin Forest Reservation.

Traffic

Bikes and horses are permitted only when snow is not on the ground but generally you will not find much competition for these trails.

Canine Swimming

There is easy access for a doggie dip at Quarry Pond and the Twin Ponds at Pine Lodge can be entered from grassy banks.

Trail Time

More than one hour.

21

Cuyahoga Valley National Park – Peninsula Depot

The Park

The Cuyahoga River takes 90 miles of twists and turns bumping into resistant rock to cover 30 miles as the proverbial crow flies. The American Indians who lived in the valley as long as 12,000 years ago called it "Ka-ih-ogh-ha," the crooked river. One of the river's severe turns creates a peninsula from which the 19th century village took its name.

When the Ohio & Erie Canal opened in 1827 Peninsula became a booming port town overnight. Four-teen bars and five hotels sprung up to service the flow of traffic on the canal. The canal era lasted a few scant decades before railroads drained their customers.

The Walks

Peninsula is an ideal starting point to experience the *Ohio & Erie Canal Towpath Trail* with your dog. Boston Store is an easy 2.5-miles to the north for a car shuttle or an out-and-back canine hike. A short distance to the south is Deep Lock Quarry with a 1.2-mile loop trail up the valley hills to the old excavation site, now liberally covered in trees. Along the way you pass Lock 28, the deepest lock on the canal, dropping the water level 17 feet, a critical linchpin in the entire waterway.

Two small trail systems are available south of Peninsula on Riverview Road, both lightly visited. The *Tree Farm Trail* off Major Road takes off from Horseshoe Pond and lopes through woods for 2.75 miles. This easy-going journey is a popular spot for moonlight snowshoe and skiing tours in the winter that your dog will likely be happy to try.

A bit further south is the Oak Hill Area with two nested loops that visit a trio of ponds and an overlook during a modest climb of some 200 feet. Although named for its oaks, the highlight of this canine hike will be the avenues through stately pines and the ravines decorated with hemlocks. The outside *Plateau Trail* provides almost five miles of rambling canine hiking.

Berea sandstone quarried here was particularly good for creating millstones.

Trail Sense: Park maps and trail maps can be picked up in the Visitor Center and at kiosks near the trailheads.

Dog Friendliness
Dogs are welcome on these trails.

Traffic
The *Towpath Trail* is too busy for a comfortable hike with your dog on good weather weekends but the hiking trails are havens of solitude most any time.

Canine Swimming
The park ponds are well-vegetated and the Cuyahoga River is not universally accessible but a water-loving dog can find a swim here.

Trail Time
More than one hour.

22

Rocky River Reservation

The Park

It all began right here. Over 21,000 acres of land, 16 reservations, more than 100 miles of parkways. The first link in Cleveland's "Emerald Necklace" was three acres of bottomland in the Rocky River Valley donated by West Side brewer Leonard Schlather in 1912.

The Cleveland park design was the vision of William A. Stinchcomb, a self-taught landscape architect and engineer in the city office who first hatched the scheme in 1905 when Cleveland was the nation's sixth largest city and most of the surrounding area still rural. The Cleveland Metropolitan Park Board was formed in 1917 and, after first volunteering his services, Stinchcomb was appointed as the first director of the Park District in 1921.

Cuyahoga County

Phone Number
- (216) 635-3200

Website
- www.clemetparks.com/visit/index.asp?action=rdetails&reservations_id=1003

Admission Fee
- None

Park Hours
- 6:00 a.m. - 11:00 p.m.

Directions
- *Many towns*; Valley Parkway runs the length of this park for 13 miles. For access in the north, take Exit 162 from I-90 to Rockcliff Lane and in the south take Exit 7 from I-480 to Mastick Road south to Cedar Point Road into the park.

He immediately set about implementing his long-ago dream and would keep at it until 1957 - a total of 58 years in public service to the city of Cleveland.

The Walks

Most of your dog's hiking day in the Rocky River valley will be spent in the Southern Section. The Northern Section features a handful of shortish loops along the parkway that can be conquered by driving a little while, hiking a little while, driving a little while...and so on. Trails visit inspiring overlooks from grassy bluffs and shale cliffs along the river.

The Southern Section also features a cornucopia of short trails, here centered around the handsome Nature Center. The most dramatic features a climb up more than 100 steps to Fort Hill that was once the outpost for Erie Indians. Once on top your dog can look back down to the Rocky River 90 feet below.

The trail system is laced with unmarked and un-mapped rogue paths so come with a mind to explore with your dog. There may be a wildflower explosion down this trail; a corridor of hem-locks down another; a frog pond at the end of that one.

Trail Sense: A detailed

This is Dunk, a 20-foot-long reproduction of a dunkleosteous, a sharklike creature who swam here when this was a warm saltwater sea.

color map is available and one can printed from the website. You will need it to find trailheads across the 13-mile park.

Dog Friendliness
Dogs are welcome on all trails and a dog bowl with water is left out at the Nature Center.

Traffic
Parking is at a premium in a popular park sometimes characterized as Cleveland's "Central Park." Vehicular traffic is limited to the park's *All-Purpose Trail*.

Canine Swimming
There are several opportunites for your dog to get into the Rocky River but swimming is not a feature of most of the trails.

Trail Time
Never more than an hour on any one trail but you can spend a day with your dog sampling all the park's hikes.

23

Goodyear Heights Metro Park

The Park

As early as 1910 Frank A. Seiberling, founder and president of Goodyear Tire and Rubber, became concerned about maintaining a highly trained, loyal work force. He proposed building a model housing community for employees.

The Goodyear board nixed the plan but Seiberling was so committed to the project that he bought land himself, choosing a rural plot of farmland just northeast of Goodyear's main plant. Seiberling hired his personal landscape architect to sculpt the grounds and included provisions for all modern conveniences like gas, electricity, and telephones.

In 1930 the company donated land for the park and Franklin Roosevelt's out-of-work "tree army," the Civilian Conservation Corps, set up camp during the Depression to develop facilities and plant tens of thousands of Scotch pines on the cropland. Over the years Goodyear Heights Metro Park has grown to 410 acres.

Summit County

Phone Number
- (440) 564-2279

Website
- www.summitmetroparks.org/ParksAndTrails/GoodyearHeights.aspx

Admission Fee
- None

Park Hours
- 6:00 a.m. to 11:00 p.m.

Directions
- *Akron*; from SR 8, exit onto Tallmadge Avenue, SR 261 and go east. Turn right on Brittain Road. Turn left on Newton Street (the Eastwood Avenue entrance is for ballfields) to the main entrance on the left. Before that, turn left on Frazier Avenue for an alternate parking lot.

The Walks

Your dog is unlikely to trot down better-groomed trails than those in this downtown park. The wide, compacted dirt-and-stone paths could stand proudly beside the fancy carriage paths of the best Catskill Mountain resorts of the 1800s. Including the sporty exercise/hiking trail there are more than five miles of such paths to fill your dog's hiking day in Goodyear Heights Metro Park.

Alder Pond Trail is a short trail that begins by going through a young forest of black cherry, red maple, red oak trees before using a boardwalk to loop through low-lying wetlands. Your dog won't see much of Alder Pond for over a mile, though. For that matter, most of the pine trees on the two-mile *Piney Woods Trail* are being muscled out by a natural succession of beech, oak and maple trees. So he won't see many of these either. Along the northern side of the trail the acidic soils support sassafras trees, whose roots were once used in making root beer before being banned by the Federal Drug Administration. Your dog will want a good drink after tackling these rolling hills. Of course, Akron is Greek for "high place," sitting at the summit of the Erie & Ohio Canal when the town was founded.

Trail Sense: A park map is posted on the information boards and trail junctions are marked. This is a simple trail system.

Dog Friendliness
Dogs are allowed on the trails and mutt mitts are provided.
Traffic
No bikes are allowed but these trails are popular with runners which means you will find trail users even far from the trailhead.
Canine Swimming
Access to Alder Pond is problematic; where the trail touches on the water there is a cement ledge.
Trail Time
More than one hour.

24

Cuyahoga Valley National Park
– Boston Store

The Park

In 1814 George Wallace built a sawmill atop of Brandywine Falls, at 67 feet the highest and most powerful waterfall in the Cuyahoga Valley. Within a decade Brandywine Village boasted a whiskey distillery, grist mill, woolen mill, and a dozen houses. The village thrived until the opening of the Ohio & Erie Canal siphoned business to the west and into boomtowns such as Boston.

Boston Store was constructed in 1836 and has been used as a warehouse, store, post office, and gathering place. Today it is a museum and a centralized base for the *Ohio & Erie Canal Towpath Trail* and Cuyahoga Valley National Park's 125 miles of trails.

Cuyahoga County

Phone Number
- (216) 524-1497

Website
- www.nps.gov/cuva/

Admission Fee
- None

Park Hours
- Sunrise to 10:00 p.m.

Directions
- *Boston*; from I-77 pick up I-271 East and exit onto SR 303, heading east. Turn left on Riverview Road before the Cuyahoga River and go 1.7 miles to Boston Mills Road. The Visitor Center is across the river.

The Walks

Falling water tumbling into the Cuyahoga valley is the dominant theme of trails around Boston Store. After a short hike north on the towpath you can pick up the *Stanford Trail* and climb easily through fields and forest to the Brandywine Creek and its signature falls. A boardwalk leads to a close observation point and the trail snakes close to the top of the foaming waters that have been grinding layers of shale for millions of years.

The trail crosses the top of Brandywine Falls and drops to the stream level where your dog can enjoy cooling waters. But if it has been raining don't bother going down since the creek crossing is on low stepping stones and impassable in high water. After circling Brandywine Creek you return back down the 1.5-mile *Stanford Trail* for a satisfying four-mile canine hike.

On the west side of the Cuyahoga River you can hike with your dog on the blue-blazed *Buckeye Trail* (or drive a short distance uphill to a small parking lot) to access the trail to Blue Hen Falls. It begins as a curving old road that winds downhill into a pleasing woodland before branching off to Spring Creek that freefalls 15 feet over a sandstone ledge. Unmarked and not noted on the park map is a rough trail that continues downstream to a more impressive hydro-spectacular - Buttermilk Falls that slides down a wall of sandstone. This route requires considerable rock hopping and splashing in shallow water which your dog certainly won't mind. Her reward is playtime in the splashpool.

Taking a break at Brandywine Falls.

Trail Sense: A park map is available and the trails are easy to follow.

Dog Friendliness
Dogs are welcome on all the trails around Boston Store.

Traffic
Boston Store is a busy place but most of the traffic, wheeled and foot, is on the *Towpath Trail*.

Canine Swimming
The best swimming is in the Cuyahoga River; the tributary streams don't have much water in them most of the year.

Trail Time
You can spend several hours on the towpath or hiking to the waterfalls. If you just want to see the plunging water you can take short hikes from parking lots.

25
Penetentiary Glen Reservation

The Park

Brothers Samuel and Salmon Halle bought out a hat and furrier shop at 221 Superior Avenue in Cleveland in 1891. Over the next several decades the Halles built a high end department store that was the rival to the prestigious signature emporiums of New York and Chicago. The company survived into the 1970s when it was sold to Marshall Field's who finally dissolved the Halle nameplate in 1982.

In 1912 Samuel Halle purchased this property as a weekend retreat and working family farm where they raised corn and hay. The park district bought 88 acres in November 1974 and added nearly 173 acres of Hallefarm in 1976 from the Halle heirs. The 424-acre park opened to the public in July of 1980.

Lake County
Phone Number - (440) 256-1404
Website - www.lakemetroparks.com/select-park/penitentiaryglen.shtml
Admission Fee - None
Park Hours - Sunrise to sunset
Directions - *Kirtland*; take Exit 193 from I-90 and head south on SR 306. Turn left on SR 615 and right on Kirtland-Chardon Road to the park entrance on the right.

The Walks

Penetentiary Glen earned its name from early settlers who found the sheer 100-foot walls of the Stony Creek gorge difficult to esacape from. Today the sandstone gorge disects the park and is visited by an easy trot on the 1-mile *Gorge Rim Loop*. This route traverses a beautiful woodland with firs along the gorge and majestic oaks elsewhere. A wooden staircase of 141 steps takes curious dogs into the gorge but only leads to a viewing platform. Hikes through the cool recesses of the gorge are limited to naturalist-led tours.

Exiting the gorge trail, the best way to see the park is along the *Bridle Trail* that circles the property in the course of three miles, alternately ducking into light woods and open fields. The wide compacted stone and natural surface

path is paw-friendly and doesn't get chewed up like some horse trails. Expansive grass areas by the trailhead are ideal for lying in the sun with your dog or a spirited game of fetch.

The history of the property is on display on the short *Halle Home Loop* that visits the remains of the one-time family farm. The only building still intact from that era is the original horse barn from 1930.

Trail Sense: Park maps, information boards and signposts make wayfinding with your dog a snap.

Dog Friendliness
Dogs are welcome to use these trails and mutt mitts are provided.

Traffic
Foot traffic only on the Gorge Rim Loop and Halle Home Loop, otherwise bikes are allowed. Horses are confined to the bridle paths. This is a busy park with easy, attractive trails.

Canine Swimming
Your dog may find a dip in an old farm pond but this is not a prime destination for your water-loving hound.

Trail Time
More than an hour possible.

26

Mentor Lagoons Nature Preserve

The Park

The charter that led to the formation of Connecticut gave the colony a sea-to-sea land grant that included the region of Northern Ohio. Even after states gave up their western claims in exchange for federal assumption of their American Revolutionary War debts, Connecticut retained more than three million acres in Ohio. The State sold the land to investors who formed the Connecticut Land Company. A surveyor from the company, Charles Parker, built the first cabin and outbuildings here on headlands that were once the riverbed of the Grand River in 1797.

Modeling their activities on successful real estate developments in Florida, the Mentor Harbor Company was created int he early 1900s with plans to dredge a harbor in the Mentor Marsh, build a private yacht club and sell housing lots for the creation of an exclusive residential community. The Depression ended those plans but some of that vision was realized in 1997 by the City of Mentor's creation of the 700-acre Mentor Lagoons Nature Preserve & Marina.

Lake County

Phone Number
- (440) 205-3625

Website
- www.cityofmentor.com/parks/lagoons.shtml

Admission Fee
- None

Park Hours
- Sunrise to sunset

Directions
- *Mentor*; take SR 2 or I-90 and exit onto 615 North, Center Street. Proceed on to Hopkins until the road ends at Lake Shore Boulevard. Turn right and then left at Harbor Drive into marina.

The Walks

This is not your everyday nature preserve. While hiking with your dog you will be as likely to dodge bikes and golf carts as you will to stop and watch migrating songbirds. The first thing dog owners need to know here is that dogs are not permitted on the *Marsh Rim Trail* and *Lakefront Loop*, which is really only a trivial inconvenience since the park's main attraction for your dog - the Lake Erie beachfront - remains on the canine hiking table.

The main route through the preserve is the *Lakefront Trail* that was once Mentor Harbor Boulevard in the 1920s. Canine hikers will make the first left onto the soft dirt *Marina Overlook Trail*, pointing towards the lake. You will have to pass the busy marina (and a fair number of Spot-A-Pots) but in a half-mile your dog will be on Lake Erie sand. You can hike a good distance down the driftwood-peppered beach before closing your loop on a wide path through a mature oak bluff forest. Watch for sheer drop-offs from the small cliffs once you lead your dog away from the beach.

Trail Sense: An information board is located at the trailhead and it may be stocked with map/brochures.

Dog Friendliness

Dogs are allowed on the trails to the west of *Lakefront Trail* and are welcome on the beach.

Traffic

Bikes and golf carts are common on the main park trails but there is less traffic in the woods and along the beach.

Canine Swimming

Absolutely. It doesn't get much better for you water-loving dog than the Lake Erie beach.

Trail Time

About one hour.

Checking out the wave action in Lake Erie at Mentor Lagoons.

27

Lakeshore Reservation

The Park

This park on the bluffs above Lake Erie was stitched together by Lake County by acquiring ten parcels of private property between 1967 and 1973. The land was targeted for development as a park because of a naturally stable sand beach and mature stands of trees.

The Walks

Of Ohio's 262 miles of Lake Erie shoreline it is estimated that only about 40 are open for access by the public - and a lot fewer than that are open to your dog so that makes this a very special place indeed for dog owners. The highlight in the 84-acre park for your dog is the driftwood-littered sandy beach that can be hiked between staircases that drop you off the bluffs. Strong swimming dogs will love the challenge of Lake Erie waves crashing onto shore.

Back on top of the bluffs the short, groomed trails in Lakeshore Reservation have a garden-like feel. The principal private landowner, Charles Irish, was a pioneering arborist

Lake County

Phone Number
- None

Website
- www.lakemetroparks.com/
select-park/lakeshore.shtml

Admission Fee
- None

Park Hours
- Sunrise to one-half hour after sunset

Directions
- *North Perry Village*; go north on Antioch Road from SR 20 in Perry and continue straight into the park.

Lakeshore Reservation gives your dog a chance to play in Lake Erie waves.

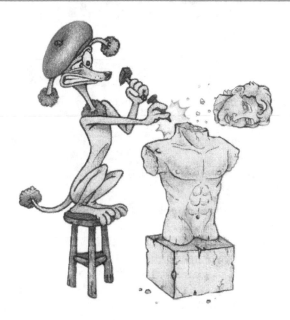

who spotted non-native ornamental trees and shrubs around his home amidst the typical Ohio beeches and maples. The park is oriented east-west and each side contains its own loop that mirror each other. The beach stroll can be used to create a canine hiking loop from side to side.

Trail Sense: The park map is posted at the information kiosk or can be printed online.

Dog Friendliness
Dogs are welcome in the park, on the beach and in the lake.
Traffic
The beach is not a sunbathing beach and the picnic areas are small so crowds are light to moderate.
Canine Swimming
Yes, but only if your dog likes waves.
Trail Time
Less than an hour of hiking time but the beach will keep your dog here longer than that.

28
Furnace Run Metro Park

The Park

Charles Francis Brush grew up on a farm 10 miles east of Cleveland but he spent less time in the fields as a boy than he did in a small wooden workshop. He was designing electricity experiments by the age of 12 and in 1878 the 29-year old Brush installed his first arc light in Cincinnati. He was the first to perfect the commercial adaptation of the arc light and his success with Brush Electric led to a merger with Edison Light to form General Electric.

Brush purchased the original grant of 2100 acres here from pioneer owner Everett Farnham to create Brushwood. The land was donated for the park in honor of his son, whose death in 1927 predated his own by two years.

Summit County

Phone Number
- (330) 865-8060

Website
- www.summitmetroparks.org/ParksAndTrails/FurnaceRun.aspx

Admission Fee
- None

Park Hours
- 6:00 a.m. -11:00 p.m.

Directions
- *Richfield*; from I-77 exit onto Brecksville Road, SR 21, and go south. Make the first right onto Townsend Road to the park entrance on the right.

The Walks

Two mirror trails, each about one mile long, spread out in the woods along the stream behind Brushwood Lake. The *Old Mill Trail* is notable for the 25-ton stone Brush family marker. The *Rock Creek Trail* loops the stream that is like a mini-Cuyahoga River with its many twists and turns.

All the canine hiking through Furnace Run is easy and suitable for any dog. The woods are pleasing and the stream beguiling but the traffic noise from adjacent I-77 doesn't foster that elusive sense of getting away from it all.

If you are looking for a place to picnic with your dog - this is it! The grassy picnic site is spotted with spruce and tall pine trees and even features a rustic Adirondack-style bench.

Trail Sense: The park map and accurate trail markings will keep you going in the right direction.

These single log dams are part of an award-winning habitat restoration project in Furnace Run.

Dog Friendliness
Dogs are welcome to hike on all three park trails.
Traffic
Foot traffic only and generally light.
Canine Swimming
There are occasional pools for paddling in Furnace Run and Brushwood Lake can host a doggie dip if not busy.
Trail Time
About one hour.

29
Buckeye Woods Park

The Park

The original park, in the west end, was a gift of Theda Schleman and is now the Schleman Nature Preserve. Additional acreage was added in the open eastern end on land that was farmed and grazed as part of the infirmary farm of the Medina County Home.

The park takes its name from elegant stands of buckeye trees that flourish in low-lying areas around the creek that flows here.

The Walks

The prime canine hiking ground in Buckeye Woods Park is in the Schleman Nature Preserve and it is a

Medina County

Phone Number
- (330) 722-9364

Website
- www.medinacountyparks.com/Pages/BuckeyeWoods.html

Admission Fee
- None

Park Hours
- 8:00 a.m to dark

Directions
- *Lafayette*; on Wedgewood Road, SR 162, a half-mile east of SR 42.

fine location to make the transition from neighborhood walks with your dog to hiking with your dog. The woods have little understory and the paths are wide and easy for your dog to trot so there is the feeling of being in the woods while still being comfortable in the "wild." There are graceful bridges over streams and wet spots so you don't have to rock hop through the water. The trails are blazed (look way up in the trees though!) so you can learn to follow a marked trail. A ridge runs down the middle of the property to give a bit of roll to the otherwise flat woodland. An ideal prescription for the beginning canine hiker.

You can also take your dog on a romp under the sun on the 1.75-mile *Chippewa Inlet Trail*, paved in asphalt and heading toward the Chippewa Nature Area There are grassy shoulders if needed as the route follows the Chippewa stream to a wetland area that was once a former peat mine. Another paved pathway in Buckeye Woods Park circles a three-acre fishing pond where your dog can cool off after a spirited jog.

Trail Sense: A map/brocure can be printed online or studied on an information board but not available on-site. The hiking trail is blazed.

Dog Friendliness
Dogs are welcome to enjoy these trails and mutt mitts are provided.
Traffic
Most of the people who come to Buckeye Woods are here for the ballfields. Bikes are not allowed in Schleman Nature Preserve.
Canine Swimming
There is vegetation around the Buckeye Woods Park pond but your dog can get in from the grassy banks for a swim.
Trail Time
An hour or more.

73

30
Mill Stream Run Reservation

The Park

Over billions of years vast deposits of pure silica, magnesia and lime were carried and deposited in Northern Ohio by the action of waves. Layer upon layer was cemented and hardened by pressure and chemical agents into some of the world's most impressive sandstone beds.

Because of the hardness of the individual grains and uniformity of grain size, sandstone, especially the trademark Berea sandstone found here, is an excellent material from which to make grindstones. By the 1870s, 400 tons of Berea sandstone were being shipped from Mill Stream Run every day, quarried by workers earning $1.50 for a 10-hour day. In the 1880s, 93% of all the world's grindstones were coming from Berea quarries, the "Sandstone Center of the World."

Mill Stream Run is the newest major reservation in the Cleveland Metropark system, opening to the public in 1976. Baldwin and Wallace lakes in the northern tip of the park are flooded sandstone quarries.

Cuyahoga County

Phone Number
- (216) 635-3200

Website
- www.clemetparks.com/visit/index.asp?action=rdetails&reservations_id=1013

Admission Fee
- None

Park Hours
- 6:00 a.m. - 11:00 p.m.

Directions
- *Strongsville*; from I-71, heading south, exit on SR 42, Pearl Road. Turn right and go 1.5 miles to the park entrance at the first traffic light past the Turnpike exit.

The Walks

The heart of canine hiking in Mill Stream Run Reservation is along Royalview Lane. At the end of the road you will find the somewhat forgotten *Big Tree Loop*. Although beleaguered by traffic noise from adjacent I-71, after a rough start this ramble picks up a paw-pleasing single-track dirt trail that culminates at a magnificent old oak that is greedily spreading its branches in the light forest. With little foot traffic, this path can become non-descript so follow your dog's nose.

The aerobic workouts of the park for trail dogs are back down the road on the stacked loops of *Royalview* and *Sugar Bush*. Each of these hikes will require about an hour for your dog to complete, visiting bottomland streams and touring wooded ravines. Again, don't be surprised if you have to negotiate an overgrown spot of trail or decipher a blowdown. After beginning on the typical ox cart-like reesrvation path the trail shifts to more traditional dirt hiking trail and back again.

Trail Sense: These trails can deteriorate to the point where standard map and junction post are insufficient but getting lost is never a worry.

Dog Friendliness
Dogs are allowed to hike these trails at Mill Stream Run.
Traffic
Away from the *All-Purpose Trail* it is possible to hike here and not see another trail user.
Canine Swimming
The streams at Royalview might provide enough water for a doggie swim; you can make special stops in the East Branch of the Rocky River for your water-loving dog.
Trail Time
More than one hour.

31
Girdled Road Reservation

The Park

European settlers learned from the Indians that the best way to remove a tree for clearing the land was to kill it by girdling, or cutting away a ring of bark completely around the trunk. This cuts off the flow of nutrients and starves the tree.

When a pioneer road from the Cleveland frontier to the Pennsylvania line became necessary so many trees were girdled to clear the path that the odd name stuck. Surveyed in 1797, this was the first road through the Western Reserve. The remaining section of the original Girdled Road is the northern boundary of the park, land for which was purchased by Lake Metroparks in 1965.

The Walks

At Girdled Road Reservation

Lake County

Phone Number
- None

Website
- www.lakemetroparks.com/select-park/girdled-road.shtml

Admission Fee
- None

Park Hours
- Sunrise to sunset

Directions
- *Concord Township*; take Exit 200 from I-90 and go south on SR 44. Turn left on Girdled Road. The North entrance is on the right side of the road in 3.5 miles. To reach the South Entrance turn right on SR 608 and go two miles to Radcliffe Road. The park entrance is on the left.

---

you can take it easy with your dog or you can take it hard. The trail system is bar-bell-shaped, standing on its end. The canine hiking loops in the park's extremes are easy trotting for your dog on compacted gravel paths. The *North Loop* is entirely a wooded affair, covering a bit more than one mile. The *Big Pond-Big Woods* loops in the south introduce more open spaces and wetlands. These successional fields attract enough avian visitation that Audubon Ohio has designated the 902-acre park an Important Bird Area.

The challenge for your dog in Girdled Road comes on the two-mile stretch of the *Buckeye Trail* that mimics the bends in Big Creek as it connects the northern and southern sections of the park. The hill-climbing here will set tongues to panting - this is the same hill that sports of a ski lift after all. The trail across the Aylworth Creek ravine is bridged and steps appear in places to ease the journey.

Trail Sense: Information boards feature park maps that can also be printed from the website.

Dog Friendliness
Dogs are allowed on the trails and throughout the park.

Traffic
Hikers only are permitted on the *Big Pond Loop*. Elsewhere you can chance to see a horse or a bike.

Canine Swimming
There is no real access to Big Creek or Aylworth Creek so steer water-loving dogs to the fishing ponds in the southern segment of the park.

Trail Time
Several hours possible.

32

Big Creek Park

The Park

Samuel Livingston Mather II could trace his roots directly back to Richard Mather who sailed to Massachusetts from England in 1635. In the 1840s his grandfather came to Ohio to dispose of family holdings in the Western Reserve. Instead, he stayed and built an empire on shipping iron ore across the Great Lakes. Mather II took his place in the family business and directed operations for two decades beginning in 1926.

In the 1920s Mather bought over 1000 acres of land here with plans to create a high class resort. His dreams were dashed by the stock market crash lurking around the corner. The land remained undeveloped and in 1955 Mather donated 505 acres to the State of Ohio. After leasing the park-

Geauga County
Phone Number - (440) 286-9516
Website - www.co.geauga.oh.us/ departments/park_district/big_ creek_park.htm
Admission Fee - None
Park Hours - 6:00 a.m.to 11:00 p.m.
Directions - *Chardon*; from I-90, take the SR 44 exit, heading south. After 3 miles turn east on Clark Road and follow it for about 2 miles. Make a right onto Robinson Road. The park entrance will be about a mile up the road at 9160.

land for 35 years, the Geauga Park District obtained ownership of Big Creek Park.

The Walks

Big Creek doesn't play a big role in your dog's hiking day in the park - depending on the trails you choose it is possible she may never see it. Instead you get "big woods." An airy beech forest, stately hemlocks, even a grove of aspens. You will cobble your dog's hiking day from several short trails.

The must-do walk here is probably the *Hemlock Trail* that slips along a high ridge above Big Creek in the distance. This is an easy, mostly flat journey for your dog, save for stairs that drop you in on one side and trail that brings you out the other.

There are about three miles of trails around the Donald W. Meyer Center, inlcuding the *Beechwoods Trail* and *Trillium Trail*, that roll across little ups and downs into gullies. The park has gone to a lot of trouble to cover its trails with stones that may help with maintenance but don't do your dog's paws any favors, knocking its rating down a peg.

Your water-loving dog will enjoy playing in the Linton Cascade at Big Creek Park.

Trail Sense: A park map/brochure is available when the center is open and trail junctions are marked with directional signs.

Dog Friendliness
Dogs are allowed to hike these trails.
Traffic
Horses are confined to the long-distance trails west of Big Creek; otherwise traffic is typically light.
Canine Swimming
The park features three fishing ponds that are not served by the trail system. The paved *Cascade Trail* leads to the Linton Cascade that spills into an ideal doggie swimming hole.
Trail Time
More than one hour.

33
Euclid Creek Reservation

The Park

Euclid Creek Watershed is not a part of a river system, but instead drains directly to Lake Erie. Industry came to Euclid Creek in the 1860s when as many as five quarries operated to extract high quality flagstones. The bustling village of Bluestone once occupied the southern part of today's park but is now a "ghost town."

The watershed has evolved over the past 100 years into one of the more highly urbanized areas along the Lake Erie coastline. But the stretch of reservation that follows Euclid Creek here remains a green oasis, first developed by the Federal government's Civilian Conservation Corps during the 1930s.

Cuyahoga County

Phone Number
- (216) 635-3200

Website
- www.clemetparks.com/visit/index.asp?action=rdetails&reservations_id=1009

Admission Fee
- None

Park Hours
- 6:00 a.m. to 11:00 p.m.

Directions
- *Richmond Heights*; take Exit 182A off I-90 and head south on Nottingham Road that becomes Dille Road and then Highland Road after crossing Euclid Avenue. Turn right into the park on Euclid Creek Parkway.

The Walks

For a narrow strip of 345 acres of parkland, Euclid Creek Reservation packs a lot of canine hiking into a small area. In fact, the park is virtually nothing beside hiking trail, road, multi-use trail, and creek squashed together side-by-side. Most dog owners will favor the wooded hillsides between Glenside Road and the Euclid Creek Parkway in the northern half of the sliver-like park. Some combination of the *Glenridge Loop Trail* and *Squirrel Run Trail* will serve up almost an hour of trail time on wide, rolling dirt paths. Your time here with your dog will immerse you completely in forests a world away from the city spreading out just past the top of the hill.

To follow Euclid Creek all the way through the reservation you will need to hop on the paved *All-Purpose Trail* with the cyclists, strollers and in-line skaters. There are places you can step off the asphalt to avoid the traffic if you need to as the trail snakes along for 2.5 miles.

A more serene option is the *Upper Highland Loop*, a balloon-style trail that mirrors Euclid Creek for a short distance past the reserved picnic area.

Trail Sense: A park map is posted at information kiosks and can be printed

Enjoying the cool riffles of Euclid Creek.

from the website. Signposts unravel the many trails traveling through the same corridor.

Dog Friendliness

Dogs are welcome to hike in the park and hang in the picnic areas. Mutt mitts are provided.

Traffic

Euclid Creek Reservation absorbs heavy use on the weekends and in good weather. The flat *All-Purpose Trail* especially will attract just about any mode of wheeled transportation that isn't motorized.

Canine Swimming

Your dog can find a splash in Euclid Creek but not much more.

Trail Time

More than one hour.

34
Black River Reservation

The Park

The Black River or Canesadooha-rie, as the native Indian tribes knew it, was famous for the number and enormity of its black bears. When hunters and trappers gave way to permanent settlers migrating from New England they put down roots here where the East and West branches merge before flowing out into Lake Erie.

The Burrell family staked out farmland on the east side of the river in 1816 and the Day family farmed the area on the west banks. The Day family soon built a dam to power a gristmill just south of today's *Bridgeway Trail* entrance. As a result most of the present park was underwater for nearly 100 years until the dam was breached.

After that the area fell into disuse until it was given to the Lorain County Metro Parks by the City of Lorain. The Black River Reservation opened to the public in 1994.

Lorain County

Phone Number
- (440) 324-5481

Website
- www.loraincountyme-troparks.com/black.htm

Admission Fee
- None

Park Hours
- Sunrise to sunset

Directions
- *Elyria*; use Exit 148 off I-90 and follow SR 254 west, that bisects the park. To reach the Day's Dam Picnic Area at the north, turn right on East River Road and left on East 31st Street. To get to Bur Oak Picnic Area, turn left on Gulf Road and immediately right on Ford Road.

The Walks

The great attraction of Black River Reservation is the 3.5-mile hike/bike *Bridgeway Trail* which runs down the spine of this 883-acre linear park passing shale cliffs, wildflower-stuffed meadows and groves of hardwoods. The highlight comes about halfway in when a 1,000 foot bridge takes canine hikers 25 feet above the river, which it crosses twice. The wide corridor the trail travels through allows dog owners ample room to step aside from wheeled traffic.

You don't need to spend your hiking day with your dog completely on blacktop. If you start at the Day's Dam Picnic Area you can take side hikes to a waterspout dropping over a shale cliff and an enormous cottonwood tree. The Black River seems to be a breeding ground for giant trees - a black walnut believed to have been the biggest tree in Ohio once grew here. Plus there are abundant grassy areas to relax with your dog or start up a game of fetch.

Cottonwood trees like this one can grow mighty big in Ohio.

The reservation's newest trail continues north from Day's Dam through the slag fields of the U.S. Steel Mill to Colorado Ave in Lorain. The trail is about 2 miles long and crosses the Black River and French Creek providing a unique study in contrasts between the natural and industrial worlds.

Trail Sense: Park maps are posted at trailhead kiosks and mile markers are posted along the way so you can pick out a length for your canine hike.

Dog Friendliness
Dogs are welcome on the trails and mutt mitts are provided.
Traffic
Any type of non-motorized, wheeled conveyance can be encountered in this popular park - estimates put the yearly visitation in the range of 500,000.
Canine Swimming
Your dog can find a way into the Black River and there are streams with pools along the *Waterfall Trail* and *Cottonwood Trail*.
Trail Time
Several hours.

35

Indian Point Park

The Park

A small sliver of 100-foot ridge pushed up between Paine Creek and the Grand River has hosted a wider diversity of cultures than just about anywhere in Northern Ohio. A tribe from the Whittlesey Culture lived in a stockade village on the high bluff 1000 years ago. Traces of two parallel earthen walls, three to five feet high, can be still be seen here, one of the earliest architectural works around Lake Erie. The tribe disappeared before European settlers arrived but their fort has landed Indian Point on the National Register of Historic Places.

In 1802 the land was deeded to the Croffot family from the Connecticut Land Company. The unique topography of the point negated much development. A boys' camp operated here for awhile and later a branch of the Knights and Ladies of Kaleva, an organization founded by Finnish emigrant John Oxelstein in 1898 to propagate the Scandanavian way of life, built a stone hut and sauna here. The hut remained intact until the 1970s, a decade after John Phelps, an ancestor of the original deedholders, sold the property to Lake County.

Lake County
Phone Number - None
Website - www.lakemetroparks.com/select-park/indian-point.shtml
Admission Fee - None
Park Hours - Sunrise to sunset
Directions - *Leroy Township*; from I-90 exit onto Vrooman Road and go north. Turn right onto Seeley Road and the park Lower Lot will be one-half mile on the left. The Upper Lot is another half-mile up the road.

The Walks

There is not much canine hiking at Indian Point but there is plenty of wonder packed into your dog's time here - overlook views in every direction, historical artifacts, great trees and swimming in the Grand River. A long staircase connects the ridgetop with the riverbed at the Point. Up top the wide, compacted gravel *Lookout Ridge Trail* makes a short loop before sloping gently towards the staircase. Along the way you'll pass under outstanding hemlocks, impressive maples and a few massive beeches. Protected overlooks of the Grand River to the north and Paine Creek to the south travel with you.

Names of campers who stayed at Indian Point 100 years ago can still be clearly read in the Totem Stone.

Down below is the confluence of Paine Creek and Grand River. The water is normally wide and shallow but in July 2006 a 500-year flood - the maximum for which the government computes statistics - sent the Grand River 11 feet above flood level, redirecting the course of Paine Creek and causing Lake County to be declared a federal disaster area.

Trail Sense: A detailed park map/brochure is available on-site and the trailheads and paths are well-marked.

Dog Friendliness
Dogs are allowed on the trails at Indian Point.

Traffic
Foot traffic only, more down below than on top but the trails beyond the picnic area are seldom crowded.

Canine Swimming
There are good times ahead for your water loving dog in the Grand River chasm or in Paine Creek.

Trail Time
More than one hour.

36
Indian Hollow Reservation

The Park

Students of history remember the great trusts of the late 1800s put together by men like John Rockefeller and Andrew Carnegie to monopolize industries like oil and steel in order to fix prices. One of the lesser known trusts was the sandstone trust. By the 1890s practically all the building sandstone in the country east of the Rocky Mountains was pulled from the ground in northern Ohio. The Grafton Stone Company that operated here - one of the best equipped quarries in the country - was in on the fix planned in 1896.The Cleveland Quarries Company continued to extract large blocks of sandstone for years to come and grindstones can still be found stacked and scattered in the western end of the park.

Lorain County

Phone Number
- (440) 458-5121

Website
- www.loraincountyme-troparks.com/indian.htm

Admission Fee
- None

Park Hours
- Sunrise to sunset

Directions
- *Grafton*; west of town from SR 57 on Parsons Road.

The land was farmed by the Sheldon family until 1963 when they donated land to Lorain County and donated other parcels. Indian Hollow Reservation opened to the public in 1975.

The Walks

The compact reservation is really two different parks separated by the East Branch of the Black River. By the parking area is a quiet picnic shelter that features open grass fields for a game of fetch or lounging about with your dog. When you are ready, take a short, curving path down to the river and cross a metal bridge into Indian Hollow's woodlands, called Sheldon Woods.

Today, Sheldon Woods is a far cry from a hundred years ago when the land was stripped clean of all vegetation for quarrymen to blast sandstone from the ground. Now it is a peaceful forest and the only stone is found compacted into the wide, paw-friendly trail that loops easily for about one mile.

The East Branch of Black River is a watery playground for your dog.

Extra hiking time with your dog can be found on rogue dirt trails that pick their way along the banks of the East Branch and wander off into the northwest section of the park, site of the most active quarries.

Trail Sense: A detailed trail map/brochure is available online and posted on the information board onsite.

Dog Friendliness
Dogs are permitted to explore the Sheldon Woods.

Traffic
Bikes are allowed on the trails; in fact, Indian Hollow is the only Lorain County Metropark that allows mountain bikes. Still, there is not much challenge here for the wheelmen and trail use is generally light.

Canine Swimming
The East Branch is wider than it is deep with small cascades to liven up your dog's play in the water.

Trail Time
About one hour.

37
Beartown Lakes Reservation

The Park

David McConoughey arrived here from Blandford, Massachusetts in 1811 to clear land and build a new life for his family. Other settlers from New England shortly followed, enough that they needed to name their small piece of the world. The pioneers could have called their settlement Raccoontown; Geauga County is named for an Indian word for raccoons, after all. Elk, deer and wolves were everywhere as well. But they picked "Beartown." One of McConoughey's sons had once killed five bruins in one day. So, it was a natural.

In 1950 Al and Jocie Bieger opened a private fishing club in Beartown, damming creeks and building a trout raceway. Suddenly Beartown had lakes. The club closed in the 1970s and Geauga County purchased the land in 1993. Three years later the 149-acre park opened.

Geauga County
Phone Number - (440) 286-9516
Website - www.co.geauga.oh.us/departments/park_district/beartown_lakes.htm
Admission Fee - None
Park Hours - Sunrise to sunset
Directions - *Beartown*; from US 422 take SR 44, Ravenna Road, south. Make your second right onto Batholomew Road and follow to its end, turning left on Quinn Road into the park.

The Walks

Canine hiking at Beartown Lakes is more about the lakes than it is the bears. Three linking trails probe the mature beech-maple woods and, of course, the open-field lakes in the park. The stony paths are not the friendliest to your dog's paws (they double as ski trails in the winter) but the attractiveness of the woodlands make up for any possible discomfort. The *Beechnut Trail* slips under large trees for almost a mile, finishing with views of Upper Bear Lake and a chance for your dog to get in and swim from a short dirt slope.

The *Whitetail Trail*, the park's longest at 1.5 miles, pushes away from the lakes and heads through the wetlands of Spring Creek to an evergreen forest. The terrain tumbles more than the other trails but never so much that your dog will collapse on one of the benches scattered along the way. The requisite all-purpose, paved trail at Beartown Lakes is the *Lake Trail* that moves through mown fields and across the dam of Lower Bear Lake.

Trail Sense: A park map is available but not needed; all trails share a common trailhead at the parking lot and signposts reliably point the way from there.

Dog Friendliness
Dogs are allowed to hike the Beartown Lakes trails.

Traffic
Horses are permitted on the *Whitetail Trail* but this is not a trail system where you will need to elbow your way around.

Canine Swimming
If the fishermen aren't out there is ample opportunity for your dog to get in a lake and practice her dogpaddle.

Trail Time
More than one hour.

38
Punderson State Park

The Park

Punderson Lake is one of the few natural lakes in Ohio. It is a kettle lake tha formed when a titanic block of ice broke off the last glacier to retreat from the state 12,000 years ago, settled down and melted into its own depression. Punderson is the largest and deepest kettle lake in Ohio.

The lake acquired the name Punderson from Lemuel Punderson who became Newbury Township's first permanent resident in 1808 and built a dam here to power a grist mill. Punderson was not so self-affected to name the lake after himself; he called it "Big Pond." The Punderson family sold off land around the lake and in the early 1900s the area was a private hunting and fishing retreat with a kennel of prized bird dogs and even a dog food factory.

The lake's economy spiraled downward during the Depression and the State of Ohio purchased the land in 1948 for hunting and fishing. In 1951, the area was transferred to the Division of Parks and Recreation for development as a state park.

Geauga County
Phone Number - (440) 564-2279
Website - www.dnr.state.oh.us/parks/punderson/tabid/780/Default.aspx
Admission Fee - None
Park Hours - 6:00 a.m. to 11:00 p.m.
Directions - *Newbury*; take Exit 27 from I-271 onto SR 87 East and follow to 11755 Kinsman Road, just west of SR 44.

The Walks

Located in the heart of Ohio's "snowbelt," Punderson is renowned as a winter sports park for sledding, snowmobiling and cross-country skiing. There is even a dedicated *Mushers Trail* for dog-sledding. The park hosts sled-dog races throughout the winter, attracting up to 65 dog teams from throughout the United States and Canada, and up to 1,000 spectators.

As such, most of the park's 14 miles of trails are not classic hiking trails. With even a hint of wet you can expect to navigate through overgrown and choppy pathways. On the positive side, the routes are roomy as they dance in and out of light woods.

Trail Sense: A park map is available and signposts mark the trailheads but don't be surprised if you encounter the occasional unmarked trail junction.

Lakes do not always translate into swims for your dog in Punderson State Park.

Dog Friendliness

Dogs are allowed on the trails and in the campground but not on the beach.

Traffic

This is a busy park but hiking is down the activity list for most visitors; you could encounter just about anything on the trail during a winter hike.

Canine Swimming

There are four lakes in the park but getting a doggie swim is problematic. There is limited access to the shore of Punderson Lake, the shores of Pine Lake are choked with vegetation and no trails go to Emerald Lake. Stump Lake offers some good swims, especially near Kinsman Road.

Trail Time

More than one hour.

39
Garfield Park
Reservation

The Park

In 1890, Cleveland officials noted that their city "stood at the foot" of major American cities with regard to its parks. A gift of 64 wooded acres by Jeptha Wade in 1884 made up the bulk of the city's paltry 103 total acres of parkland.

In 1893, the Ohio legislature authorized the City to issue $800,000 in bonds to develop large parks in seven districts of Cleveland. $33,000 of that money was spent to buy 157 acres for Newburg Park. The higher elevation here was considered healthier than the swampy, diesase-ridden areas of the Cuyahoga River and the south side park quickly became a popular getaway. In 1986 the park was leased to Cleveland Metroparks and carries on today as Garfield Park.

Cuyahoga County

Phone Number
- (216) 635-3200

Website
- www.clemetparks.com/visit/index.asp?action=rdetails&reservations_id=1010

Admission Fee
- None

Park Hours
- 6:00 a.m. to 11:00 p.m.

Directions
- *Garfield Heights*; from I-480 exit at Broadway Avenue, SR 14 and turn right (north). Continue to the park entrance on the left. For Mill Creek Falls, continue straight on Garfield Park Boulevard to Turney Road. Turn right and go one mile to the traffic light at Warner Road. Turn left to the Visitor Center on the right.

The Walks

Most visitors to Garfield Park stick to the two-mile, paved loop trail that circumnavigates the reservation. This is an easy circuit for your dog, save for a pair of long hills. There are plenty of trees to keep the asphalt cool on your dog's paws in the summer sun.

You can escape the crowds with your dog by descending into the area around Wolf Creek that made up the heart of old Newburg Park. The premier route is the *Iron Springs Loop*, named after a once gushing Iron Spring where visitors once lapped up the rusty water for its supposed healing powers. Expect detours from restoration of the meticulous stoneworking around the Old Boating Pond. You can return to the *All-Purpose Trail* via the *North Ravine*

Bonus

The Solar System Walk is a stretch of the
All-Purpose Trail that illustrates the enormity of the
earth's solar system through the use of signs.
Don't forget, a dog, Laika, was the first living
creature to orbit the Earth. To start the Solar System
Walk, follow Wolf Creek west to Trolley Turn picnic
area, approximately one mile west of the
Broadway Avenue entrance.

Loop that reaches into the mature woods of a stream-cut gully.

The *Mill Creek Connector* leads down a neighborhood road to Cuyahoga County's highest waterfall, Mill Creek Falls. There is a small park and history center at the falls, but no playing in the plunge pool for your dog. In the 1800s, water from the falls powered so many lumber and grain mills that Newburgh was a larger city than Cleveland. When water power became obsolete the railroads actually moved the falls into a different part of the gorge in 1905.

Trail Sense: Park maps are posted at information kiosks and signposts identify trail junctions.

Dog Friendliness
Dogs are permitted across the park.

Traffic
Bikes, strollers, rollerbladers all use the busy all-purpose trail; not so many trail users dip into the wooded ravine.

Canine Swimming
No, there isn't enough water in the park to host canine aquatics.

Trail Time
About one hour.

40
Tinker's Creek State Park

The Park

Glaciers from the last Ice Age during the Pleistocene era 10,000 years ago that are responsible for most of Ohio's terrain had a particularly future-shaping impact here. This part of Ohio is known for its large number of kettle lakes, formed when blocks of ice broke free from the retreating ice sheet and melted.

More important was the piling of glacial debris that made this one of the highpoints of the state and a natural watershed divide. To the north the Cuyahoga River flowed into Lake Erie and rainfall on the southern side drained into the Tuscarawas and the Ohio River. Only an 8-mile overland portage was necessary to canoe from Lake Erie to the Ohio River - and the Gulf of Mexico for that matter, making this stretch of land an important trade center for American Indians and European settlers.

For many years this area of small kettle lakes was a private park known as Colonial Spring Gardens. The State of Ohio purchased the land in 1966 and developed a state park and nature preserve.

Portage County
Phone Number - (440) 564-2279
Website - www.dnr.state.oh.us/parks/ tinkers/tabid/793/Default.aspx
Admission Fee - None
Park Hours - Sunrise to sunset
Directions - *Streetsboro*; take Exit 41 off I-480 and head east. Make an immediate left onto Aurora-Hudson Road and follow it north, taking the right bend in the road to the park entrance on the left.

The Walks

As befits a park whose mandate is to maintain its original state as a swamp and marshland, canine hiking on the natural trails that encircle the ponds and lakes can be a squishy affair. Your dog sure won't mind but you may want to put off a visit until a drought. There are almost four miles of easy-going, flat trails in the park, wide enough to host cross-country skiing in the winter.

The swamps and marshlands intrude on the trail at times and maintenance can be iffy but you quickly put the developed part of the park behind on this tour with your dog. The frogs and geese and ducks on display will be certain to keep your dog's tail wagging here.

Trail Sense: A map/ brochure is avalaible but if one can't be had onsite, just head for the lake and start walking around. Or aim for the far end of the parking lot and head down the *Pond Run Trail*. Even though the trailheads and paths aren't marked you will find your way around.

Dog Friendliness
Dogs are allowed to use the trails in Tinker's Creek State Park but are not allowed in the adjoining Tinker's Creek State Nature Preserve.

Traffic
Most people come to the park for the playground or to drop a line into the spring-fed lake or one of the ponds; far fewer brave these primitive trails. Most hikers are heading for the nature preserve next door.

Canine Swimming
A swim for your dog is a good way to clean off paws before getting back in the car and the lakes and ponds will do just fine.

Trail Time
More than one hour.

41
Chagrin River Park
Lake County
On Reeves Road, off Lost Nation Road, just north of SR 2.

The Chagrin River that forms the park's southern boundary has proven a treasure trove for seekers of prehistoric culture. Several excavations over the years have uncovered artifacts including clay vessels, bird bone beads, projectile points, scrapers, and a large number of smoking or ceremonial pipes. The park was formed when Lake Metroparks purchased 101 acres here in 1993.

As crushed stone, multi-use trails go, this is one of the best to hike with your dog. There are almost three miles of such paths, essentially in two loops on either side of the Chagrin River, linked by a pedestrian bridge. The trails adhere to the river at every opportunity, often festooned with spring wildflowers. There is easy access to the the river for your dog to play and splash in the shallow, frisky waters. The park even turns a powerline corridor into a positive, serving up views of wavy grasses when the *Riverwood Loop* passes under the wires.

42
Hudson Springs Park
Summit County
On Stow Road, just north of SR 303 in Hudson.

Hudson Springs is the centerpiece of the town of Hudson's more than 1000 acres of parkland. And the park's centerpiece is a 50-acre lake that is wrapped inside a 1.8-mile crushed limestone path and ringed by mature woodland. Your best trail companion will enjoy trotting along the appealing curvy trail but the real reason to bring your dog here is the dog park located down the north side of the lake. There is a large, unfenced grass area for your dog to romp and easy access to the water from a grassy bank. Easy hiking and a great swim - that's a good day for any dog.

For extended trail time cross Stow Road and take another crushed limestone path through Bicentennial Woods, one of the few remaining hardwood forests still standing in Hudson.

43
Princess Ledges Nature Preserve

Medina County

In Grafton, on Spruce Road on the west side of Pearl Road and north of Grafton Road.

This area was subdivided in the 1920s to create summer cottage lots but when the economy collapsed sales withered and many properties were given away as prizes in local movie theaters. The underlying sandstone made it difficult to do much with the land and Medina County began acquiring pieces for a nature preserve in 1973, taking its name from the daughter of one of the landowners. Princess always like playing on the sandstone ledges.

The trail system in the park, in dense, undisturbed forest, is a stacked loop with the longest route sliding downhill and back over one mile. It is a good place to go and hike alone with your dog. The smaller loop is the *Ledges Trail* that moves easily along the limestone outcroppings. This route is suitable for any level of canine hiker - no scary dropoffs or intimidating passages.

Playing among the more than 1,000 feet of ledges in the nature reserve.

44
Big Creek Reservation
Cuyahoga County
On Big Creek Parkway, south of I-480 via Tiederman Road and Brookpark Road.

Lake Isaac, a pothole from the last Ice Age, is the cown jewel of Big Creek Reservation. The trail around the lake, however doesn't pay much attention to the water after leaving the trailhead. The pretty woodland becomes the star. The typical wide Metropark limestone path doesn't seem as wide as usual as it tunnels through the understory and passes close to the oaks and maples.

To the west, via Main Street is another easy canine hike around a lake, this one Beyer's Pond. This smaller body of water is more of a fishing hole than its waterfowl refuge neighbor. This path is woodchip and dirt and spills in and out of light woods and open spaces around the wetlands.

There is no need to bother with the 8-mile *All-Purpose Trail* that travels down the middle of residential Big Creek Parkway; hiking with your dog here is like going for a neighborhood walk.

45
Frohring Meadows
Geauga County
Southeast of Chagrin Falls via SR 9, Chagrin Road and left on Savage Road.

Paul Frohring, a biochemist and pioneer in nutritional supplements, donated 176 acres of farmland to the Geauga Park District in 1996 providing the spark for this unique community park. After generations of nurturing soybeans, oats, corn and wheat the abandoned farm fields provided the incubator for a special habitat creation project featuring a 100-acre tall grass prairie. When this array of grass species matures your dog will be able to trot through this part of Ohio as it appeared in the early days of settlement. A paved pathway leads through the wet prairie on the *Dragonfly Trail*.

A longer *Big Bluestem Trail* runs for an hour through meadowland and upland forest and hosts foot traffic in the summer and cross-country skiing in the winter.

46
Burton Wetlands Nature Preserve

Geauga County

Southwest of Burton on Pond Road via Rapids Road from Kinsman Road, SR 87.

Melting glaciers left mounds of layered sand and gravel known as kame and blocks of ice that melted to form depressions called kettles. This souvenir landscape of the Ice Age has been recognized as a National Natural Landmark. As you tread lightly with your dog look for rare plants such as woodland orchids, tamarack trees and cranberries.

It takes a special plant to make a life in a nutrient-challenged environment like the White Pine Bog Forest. Some have evolved to draw their sustenance from juicy insects. The wood bog around Lake Kelso at the end of the *Glacier Trail* is a good place to observe these insectivorious plants. Ewer- shaped pitcher plants lure insects with the promise of a sweet nectar meal from which they slip into a deadly trap for consumption by a cocktail of digestive fluids in the pitcher. Tiny hairs pointing downward prevent the doomed victims from crawling to freedom.

The rolling one-mile *Kettle Trail* explores this kame-and-kettle topography, first through grass-and-clover mown paths, a hardwood forest and, finally, a beaver-influenced wetland.

This floating observation deck affords sweeping views of Lake Kelso.

47
Rising Valley Recreation Area
Summit/Medina County
Northeast of Richfield on Oviatt Road, north of Center Road, SR 303.

The federal government turned over land for this 227-acre park to Richfield and Hinckley Townships. On the flat land ballfields were built and the slopes were left forested. A trail system with two nested loops was created.

The *Red Trail* scoots along and down and up gullies. This narrow band of path is unmaintained (leafy twigs will be snapping under your dog's paws) and if your dog isn't picking up the route look for logs laid along the trail that may still be there. When you are not scouting the trail, also look for large boulders scattered in the woods, glacial erratics that are souvenirs of the Ice Age that helped form these ravines.

The *Blue Trail* is an odd canine hike that drops down a long sledding hill towards the East Branch of the Rocky River but never reaches the water before heading back up the opposite side. This path is grass all the way and may not be mown and may not be dry - neither of which will concern your trail dog in the least but can annoy you.

48
Sunny Lake Park
Portage County
Southeast of Aurora on East Mennonite Road, east of South Chillicothe Road, SR 43.

Sunny Lake Park is a typical town/community open space with picnic tables and a paved exercise path. It rises above similar outings for your dog for several reasons. Most obviously, the multi-use trail surrounds a lake and the mostly open route affords almost constant water views. The 1.8-mile loop gives your dog an acceptable workout.

The park is also graced by a Bicentennial Memorial Tree Garden. Planted only in 1999, most of the trees are still eye-high making it easy to appreciate the many varieties of conifer and hardwoods on display. And to top it off for dog owners there is the Tails 'n Trails Dog Park around the corner on Page Road. The off-leash area is bounded by an attractive wooden rail fence but there is no shade.

49
Whitlam Woods

Geauga County
Northwest of Hambden at 12500 Pearl Road, west of Old State Road, SR 608.

If you are looking for an attractive woods to spend on a hiking trail with your dog where you won't have to worry about bikes or horses or most likely any other trail users for that matter, Whitlam Woods is a good call. In 1959, Fred Whitlam sold property and gave the proceeds to Geauga County with the stipulation that the money be used to purchase woodland to be held as a memorial forest for "pioneers of the Western Reserve."

The woodland here would make Fred Whitlam proud. Towering hemlocks decorate the ravines (crossed by an elaborate wooden bridge/staircase) and a climax beech-maple forest shade a lush understory. The *Sugarbush Trail* is the marquee ramble for your dog here, a rolling exploration along the edge of steep gullies.

50
Bessie Benner Metzenbaum Park

Geauga County
Southwest of Chesterland on Cedar Road via Chillicothe Road, SR 306.

The story goes that James Metzenbaum, a prominent Cleveland attorney, was out driving one sleepless night in the 1940s and discovered this property with a 140-foot knoll looming over the Griswold Creek bottomlands. He purchased the land as a memorial for his wife Bessie, who had died several years earlier and called it Wisteria Hill. He never lived here but used the property as a camp for children and later the Metzenbaum School. The county park opened in 1992.

Three short trails probe this small but engaging park, the most prominent being the *Summit Trail* that scales that knoll on a compacted stone path. Only a half-mile, your dog is sure to get a

This hollow tree is a landmark on the **Summit Trail.**

workout here. Once down from the knoll, all-access trails visit the remains of an old orchard, two conifer plantations and the wetlands of Griswold Creek.

Camping With Your Dog In The Cleveland Region

Country Lakes Family Campground
Montville
On SR 6, east of SR 528.
RV/tent   open late April to early October   **(440) 968-3400**
www.countrylakescampground.com

Heritage Hills Campgrounds
Thompson
At 6445 Ledge Road from SR 528 south of I-90, Exit 212.
RV/tent   open May 1 to October 1   **(440) 298-1311**

Punderson State Park
Newbury
East of town on the south side of SR 87.
RV/tent   open year-round   **(440) 564-1195**
www.dnr.state.oh.us/parks/punderson/tabid/780/Default.aspx

Windrush Hollow
Huntsburg
At 15560 Mayfield Road, US 322, west of town.
RV/tent   open May 1 to October 15   **(440) 635-5050**

Lorain County

American Wilderness Campground
Grafton
At 17273 Avon Beldon Road (SR 83), south of SR 303, southeast of town
RV/tent   open May 15 through October 31   **(440) 926-3700**
www.americanwildernesscampground.com

Pier-Lon Park Family Campground

Medina

West of town at 5960 Vandemark Road, north of Chatham Road, SR 162, via Lafayette Road, SR 42.

RV/tent   **open April 15 to October 21**   (330) 441.1778

www.pier-lonpark.com

Shawnee Lake Park

Spencer

East of town at 6464 Congress Road, south of SR 162.

RV/tent   **open May 1 to October 15**   (330) 648-2577

www.shawneelakepark.com

Sunset Lake Campground

Spencer

West of PA 60, Exit 14 at 6138 Tuscarawas Road.

RV/tent   **open May 1 to October 15**   (330) 667-2686

www.sunsetlakecampground.com

Willow Lake Park

Brunswick

At 2400 Substation Road, southwest of town from SR 42 via SR 303 and left.

RV/tent   **open May 1 to late October**   (330) 225-6580

www.willowlakepark.net

Country Acres Campground
Ravenna
West of town via SR 5 to SR 225 to 9850 Minyoung Road.
RV/tent   open late April to mid-October   (330) 358-2774
www.countryacrescamping.com

Jellystone Park Camp Resort
Mantua
Northeast of town on SR 82, two miles west of SR 44.
RV/tent   open mid-May to mid-October   (330) 562-9100
www.jellystoneohio.com

Streetsboro/Cleveland SE KOA
Streetsboro
West of town on SR 303.
RV/tent   open mid-May to mid-October   (330) 650-2552
www.streetsborokoa.com

West Branch State Park
Ravenna
On Rock Springs Road, south of SR 5 east of town.
RV/tent   open year-round   (330) 296-0638
www.dnr.state.oh.us/tabid/795/default.aspx

Woodside Lake Park
Streetsboro
At 2486 Frost Road, northeast of town, north of SR 303.
RV/tent   open April 15 to October 15   (330) 626-4251
www.woodsidelake.com

Summit County

Silver Springs Campground
Stow
At 5238 Young Road via Norton Road east of SR 91.
RV/tent   open mid-April to late October   (330) 689-5100
www.stow.oh.us/Departments/ParksRecreation/campgrounds.shtml

Index to Parks Around Cleveland...

As a young lawyer, 19th century Senator George Graham Vest of Missouri, addressed the jury on behalf of his client, suing a neighbor who had killed his dog. Vest's speech has come to be known as "Tribute to the Dog."

The best friend a man has in the world may turn against him and become his enemy. His son or daughter that he has reared with loving care may prove ungrateful. Those who are nearest and dearest to us, those whom we trust with our happiness and our good name may become traitors to their faith. The money that a man has, he may lose. It flies away from him, perhaps when he needs it most. A man's reputation may be sacrificed in a moment of ill-considered action. The people who are prone to fall on their knees to do us honor when success is with us may be the first to throw the stone of malice when failure settles its cloud upon our heads.

The one absolutely unselfish friend that man can have in this selfish world, the one that never deserts him, the one that never proves ungrateful or treacherous is his dog. A man's dog stands by him in prosperity and in poverty, in health and in sickness. He will sleep on the cold ground, where the wintry winds blow and the snow drives fiercely, if only he may be near his master's side. He will kiss the hand that has no food to offer; he will lick the wounds and sores that come in an encounter with the roughness of the world. He guards the sleep of his pauper master as if he were a prince. When all other friends desert, he remains. When riches take wings, and reputation falls to pieces, he is as constant in his love as the sun in its journey through the heavens.

If fortune drives the master forth an outcast in the world, friendless and homeless, the faithful dog asks no higher privilege than that of accompanying him, to guard him against danger, to fight against his enemies. And when the last scene of all comes, and death takes his master in its embrace and his body is laid away in the cold ground, no matter if all other friends pursue their way, there by the graveside will the noble dog be found, his head between his paws, his eyes sad, but open in alert watchfulness, faithful and true even in death.

Other Books On Hiking With Your Dog from Cruden Bay Books
www.hikewithyourdog.com

DOGGIN' THE MID-ATLANTIC: *400 Tail-Friendly Parks To Hike With Your Dog In New Jersey, Pennsylvania, Delaware, Maryland and Northern Virginia - $18.95*
DOGGIN' PITTSBURGH: *The 50 Best Places To Hike With Your Dog In Southeast Pennsylvania - $12.95*
DOGGIN' THE POCONOS: *The 33 Best Places To Hike With Your Dog In Pennsylvania's Northeast Mountains - $9.95*
DOGGIN' THE BERKSHIRES: *The 33 Best Places To Hike With Your Dog In Western Massachusetts - $9.95*
DOGGIN' NORTHERN VIRGINIA: *The 50 Best Places To Hike With Your Dog In NOVA - $9.95*
DOGGIN' DELAWARE: *The 40 Best Places To Hike With Your Dog In The First State - $9.95*
DOGGIN' MARYLAND: *The 100 Best Places To Hike With Your Dog In The Free State - $12.95*
DOGGIN' JERSEY: *The 100 Best Places To Hike With Your Dog In The Garden State - $12.95*
DOGGIN' RHODE ISLAND: *The 25 Best Places To Hike With Your Dog In The Ocean State - $7.95*
DOGGIN' THE FINGER LAKES: *The 50 Best Places To Hike With Your Dog - $12.95*
DOGGIN' CONNECTICUT: *The 57 Best Places To Hike With Your Dog In The Nutmeg State - $12.95*
DOGGIN' LONG ISLAND: *The 30 Best Places To Hike With Your Dog In New York's Playground - $9.95*
DOGGIN' THE TIDEWATER: *The 33 Best Places To Hike With Your Dog from the Northern Neck to Virginia Beach - $9.95*
DOGGIN' THE CAROLINA COASTS: *The 50 Best Places To Hike With Your Dog Along The North Carolina And South Carolina Shores - $11.95*
DOGGIN' AMERICA'S BEACHES: *A Traveler's Guide To Dog-Friendly Beaches - (and those that aren't) - $12.95*
THE CANINE HIKER'S BIBLE - $19.95
A Bark In The Park: *The 55 Best Places To Hike With Your Dog In The **Philadelphia Region** - $12.95*
A Bark In The Park: *The 50 Best Places To Hike With Your Dog In The **Baltimore Region** - $12.95*
A Bark In The Park: *The 37 Best Places To Hike With Your Dog In **Pennsylvania Dutch Country** - $9.95*

1894366